The Abuse of Care in Residential Institutions

Other SCA Co-publications

Residential Care: An International Reader
Meir Gottesman

The Children Act: A Social Care Guide
Ian Mallinson

Quality Counts: Achieving Quality in Social Care Services
Des Kelly and Bridget Warr (Editors)

Social Care: Rivers of Pain, Bridges of Hope
Leonard Davies

Yesterday's Answers:
Development and Decline of Schools for Young Offenders
Jim Hyland

Insights into Inspection:
The Regulation of Social Care
Roger Clough

Keyworking in Social Care:
A Structured Approach to Provision
Ian Mallinson

Care Management and the New Social Work:
A Critical Analysis
Michael Sheppard

Changing Social Care: A Handbook for Managers
Des Kelly and John Harris

Forthcoming:

Coping with Violence
Vaughan Bowie

Social Care: An Introductory Reader
Des Kelly and Chris Payne

A Whiting & Birch Ltd / SCA (Education) Co-Publication

The Abuse of Care in Residential Institutions

edited by

Roger Clough

Whiting and Birch Ltd

MCMXCVI

Published by Whiting & Birch Ltd,
PO Box 872, London SE23 3HL, England.
USA: Paul & Co, Publishers' Consortium Inc, PO Box 442, Concord, MA 01742.

British Library Cataloguing in Publication Data.
A CIP catalogue record is available from the British Library

ISBN 1 871177 93 6 (cased)
ISBN 1 871177 94 4 (limp)

Printed in England by Antony Rowe, Chippenham

Contents

Foreword

The fact that some older people are abused within residential care homes and nursing homes is being recognised, perhaps belatedly. Such abuse of vulnerable people is hard to contemplate and accept: too often we prefer to close our eyes, in part because a recognition of the problem makes a compelling demand for action.

The papers in this book are the product of a conference held at Lancaster University in the summer of 1995. However, they have been written as chapters for a book, to develop particular themes. Thus, in places there are references to 'the Lancaster Conference'.

We believe that this was the first national conference focusing on abuse of older people in the twin sectors of residential and nursing care provision. The richness of this collection is a consequence of working across the health and welfare divide.

But if the predecessor of this book is the conference, the predecessor of the conference is the concerns of two people, John Osborne and Mandy Stott as they recognised, faced and tackled abuse in a residential home. They wanted to examine their concerns in a wider forum; but they also wanted to highlight a topic that seemed to them too neglected. Olive Stevenson worked with them and I joined their group at a later stage. The conference - and this book - was triggered by their persistence.

In an edited book there are too many people to acknowledge individually. Each of us as authors knows the extent to which we have gained from support of family, friends and colleagues. We hope that they know that too.

David Whiting and Diana Birch from the publishers supported the publication from its early days - and enabled us to get from manuscript to finished product in six months.

Abuse of older people in places designed to provide care is scandalous. It must be recognised. And it must be stopped. As Olive Stevenson reminds us, nobody should take the whole burden of the failings of provision on individual shoulders: such a way leads to guilt and immobilisation. Yet we can, and I suggest must, do something. We hope that this book will contribute to the recognition of abuse - and to the necessary action.

Roger Clough
Lancaster
February 1996

Part One:

The Nature of the Task

One

The abuse of residents

Roger Clough

INTRODUCTION

The cruelty that thrives on secrecy is how *The Independent* (1994) in a leading article described abuse in residential homes. How does it happen that in the very places where people have gone for care they find themselves abused by others? At the centre of the concern about the abuse of people in residential homes and nursing homes lies a terrifying reality: in such homes it is not possible to guarantee even the minimum that people will not be abused. It is tempting to use increasingly powerful words to describe the awfulness of such events. There is no doubt that, frequently, such words would be justified. Yet constant repetition of the horrors may contribute little to the understanding either of the reasons how and why abuse occurs, or of why abuse is not stopped.

In this book we set out some of the background, examining what is known about abuse in nursing and residential care homes. There are no inclusive words which neatly can be used to describe both residential care and nursing homes, the people who live there, nor the style of life. So we write of establishments, homes, Homes, facilities and institutions. The last of these, 'institution', is used as a neutral term, not to suggest that the places are necessarily institutional in the sense that they adopt regimes which suit the running of the establishment rather than the wants and needs of the residents. Of course, some places may be institutional in just that sense. On occasions, authors make specific reference to residential care homes or to nursing homes.

We write also of 'residents' and 'users', and I know of no better phrase than 'residential life' to describe the life style though am aware that this is not the phrase that would be commonplace in nursing homes.

The book should be seen as introductory to the topic of abuse in homes for older people. The authors attempt to set the scene for an examination of abuse in terms of: nature and definition; scale and prevalence; relationship to the core tasks in homes; explanations; the work environment; establishing good standards of care; taking action to prevent abuse or investigate allegations. Thus, we do not attempt a comprehensive overview of abuse in such institutions. In particular, we have not set out to present specific detail on drawing up guidance to tackle abuse. Further work in research and analysis is imperative.

It will become apparent that the different authors do not speak with one voice. The most striking example of this is found with various comments of what comprises abuse: Mike Nolan considers that the term should include everyday poor practice, George Mabon argues that the word implies intent, a perspective questioned by Olive Stevenson; Roger Clough highlights the dangers of using the word indiscriminately for anything that falls short of the best practice. Nor do individuals necessarily subscribe to the views of others, for example as to whether or not over the years there have been improvements to the quality of life of older people in homes.

SECRECY AND IGNORANCE

Abuse thrives on secrecy. One consequence is that there is no firm evidence of the scale of abuse. The revelations that are highlighted by investigations turn back the curtain, allowing us to glimpse what is going on behind. There is a temptation to assume that abuse is widespread on the grounds that there are too many revelations for that not to be the case. However, there is another temptation to which owners and managers in all sectors are prone, which is to denounce the specific abuse that is reported but to state that such abuse is not typical of most establishments. The reality is that we have limited information on the scale of abuse in nursing homes and residential homes. This is one of the by products of secrecy.

That is not to say that we know nothing. Some work has been done both in the UK and in the United States to study the prevalence of different types of abuse in different types of homes and that information is reported here. Frank Glendenning makes a significant contribution to our knowledge base; further studies are reported in Mike Nolan's chapter.

DEFINITION OF ABUSE

I have already pointed to the differences in definitions of abuse that are taken, even in this book. The debate as to what is and is not to be termed 'abuse' must continue because it is important that the word has a clear meaning, though it is necessary to move rapidly to an agreed definition. Whatever the outcome of that debate, there must be no tolerance of practice that demeans older people. This is not to ascribe to individual staff members blame for bad practice but to state that poor practice will not be accepted.

In the rest of this section I put forward a personal perspective on definition. Most writing on abuse relates to abuse in households: violence and assaults from one adult to another or from adult to child. There has been analysis of three main categories of abuse: abuse of children; abuse of women by adult partners; and abuse of dependent adults, in particular of older people and those with learning disabilities. Some definitions are so inclusive that it becomes difficult to examine a coherent subject or to take appropriate action. Thus some people include taking financial advantage or theft under the banner of abuse (Eastman, 1993), while others categorise as 'abuse' the failure of governments to produce policies which will prevent people being poor or cold or without enough to eat. There is no doubt that these are abusive situations. Several authors in this study highlight the significance of structures in establishing the preconditions for abuse.

Yet there are dilemmas created by this all inclusive terminology (Clough, 1995). There are some who would argue that writing about 'abuse' allows the seriousness and frequently the inherent criminality to be diluted: a crime is dealt with as abuse. The debate is examined in this volume by Ann Craft as well as elsewhere (Clough, 1995).

I contend that there are three key points in determining language appropriate to the event. The terminology must lead to: accurate analysis; due weight attached to the seriousness of the event for it must not be belittled; and action becoming more rather than less likely. On these grounds I would reserve the word 'abuse' for events that both are serious and that have a direct effect on the physical and emotional well-being of the resident: physical assault, sexual assault and cruelty (including physical and emotional neglect). I exclude stealing from residents because I think the motivation and responses differ from other abusive situations. Thus it is necessary to distinguish acts of unkindness from abuse. Such acts may well be on the same continuum as acts that I shall term abuse but I want to ensure that proper consideration is given to the most serious of events. Indeed, it may be helpful also to distinguish 'an abusive environment' from 'abuse to a person'. In residential care and nursing homes, an abusive environment is one where the organisation of life in the home demeans the people who live there and creates the preconditions for individual acts of abuse to residents.

DIFFERENT EXPLANATIONS OF ABUSE

Various explanations have been developed in the field of domestic abuse, which are summarised by Rowlings (1995). Adapting her structure, these may be termed:

Structural
Older people are held in low esteem and receive poor services; there is little concern with the welfare of older people; indeed, the low status of older people in general will be compounded for older people who are dependent on others for care;

Environmental
The environments in which dependent adults live and in which carers undertake care, create stresses that are intolerable: this affects the behaviour of adult and carer, which leads to abuse;

Individual characteristic
People with particular personality types or with particular histories (perhaps of being out of control or of being abused by others) are more likely to abuse than others.

Some explanations are less threatening to our own identity than others. If I adopt a view that it is particular types of people who abuse others (and if I do not see myself in the categories of those personality types) then I construct abuse as something that not only is done by others but will only be done by others. Whereas if I acknowledge that environmental factors may play a part in producing abusive situations I may no longer be able to see myself as someone who could never abuse people. Am I to consider that an act which is a gross violation of trust and significant abuse of another is one that in certain circumstances and because of the person whom I am, I might commit? Most of the time we presume fundamentals about ourselves: that we do not have it in us to murder or to abuse our children. As residential workers we are likely to presume also that because we know that we are in the business of residential work for the welfare of others we could not, as well as would not, abuse residents. We might be falsely accused of such an event, but we have confidence that we would not perpetrate it.

COMPARISON TO DOMESTIC ABUSE

It should not be assumed that analysis of domestic abuse is translatable into residential homes. There are factors that are intrinsic to residential life and these must form part of the analysis of residential abuse. The first is that residential work by nature of its task requires staff to be involved in the intimate physical care of people who are not their intimates. Therefore we must examine the motivation of staff and the ways in which boundaries are established which allow them to enjoy the physical care of others without setting their own needs above those of the residents. In other words we need to be sure that there is proper closeness and intimacy, since without that, care is sterile. But we have to ensure also that vulnerable people are treated with respect and dignity.

The second factor relates to the organisation of the environment in which people live. The manner in which the institution is run (or managed) has immense significance for the lives of the people who live there and for those who work there. By this is meant both the systems that are established formally for the carrying out of the basic tasks for which the establishment exists and the informal systems which are so influential on what people do. To what extent do the structures, perhaps insidiously, allow abuse to develop? alternatively, may structures themselves be abusive? Within homes, the environmental explanation outlined above has an additional component: the way in which the organisation with responsibility for the management of the home influences the daily life of residents through the systems it adopts and its own set of values in relation to the tasks undertaken. These themes are discussed by Elizabeth Henderson, Lorayne Ferguson, Mark Lymbery and Dick Clough.

Thirdly, it is imperative to assess the significance of the

standing of older people in our society. To what extent is abuse more likely because the lives of older people, in particular of those who demonstrably cannot manage without help, are held in less worth than those of children or younger adults? We do not do justice to this theme but recognise its significance for the construction of the environments of older people who live in homes: the quality of the building (space, fittings); the values ascribed to the work by those outside as well as those working within homes; the management of the daily interaction between resident and staff. Evelyn McEwen's chapter is a powerful reminder of this.

ACTION: THE CONFRONTING OF ABUSE

From this, we move to action:

- to what extent may staff training and organisational structure promote good practice and limit abuse?
- what inhibits staff from telling others when things go wrong?
- how are enquiries conducted?

In turn, George Mabon, Jill Manthorpe and Dick Clough set the scene for examining these topics. There is immense pressure on people in their own place of work and their lives as a whole to maintain the status quo. Some writers on systems have used the word homeostasis to describe this force, the striving of a system to maintain a steady state. Thus it is reasonable to view the residential establishment as a system which strives to perpetuate its existence. In this sense, different parties have an interest in excluding factors that threaten the home. So it is not surprising to find that at times people who raise questions about practice may not be seen as knights in shining armour but as trouble makers. It is readily apparent that management may adopt this stance. What is less obvious is that the rest of us may do the same: as relatives, professionals, lay members of society, we may not want to face what we may see if we pull back the curtain.

As stated earlier, we do not set out to specify the details of the actions that should be taken following allegations of abuse. The reason for this is twofold: some agencies have good procedures which have been developed in collaboration with other local organisations; secondly, we are considering underlying factors. For example, a seemingly good code of practice may not result in people raising their doubts if there is limited understanding of why people are unwilling to 'tell tales' or why within organisations such messages may not be welcome.

The reason is related to an understanding of systems and cultures together with notions of loyalty, responsibility and accountability. If we learn from an early age that it is good not to tell tales, how are we to re-learn this? It is reasonable that a staff member should behave as a responsible member of the establishment and the organisation which manages it. What are the implications of this in daily life? Our hope is that by unpicking some of these matters it will be more likely that any person will both know that their prime responsibility is to the person who lives in the home and act in accord with such knowledge by working out how to question when there is unease.

One particular way in which allegations are examined is through investigation by managers, inspectorates or outsiders. Any investigation creates immense stress. Staff rationally may want any allegation to be examined; emotionally they may be resentful of the stresses under which they work on a day to day basis or upset that the quality of their work into which they have put so much effort should be questioned. Given a continuation of current trends there will be an increase in investigations. There is limited review of what constitutes good practice in such investigations. Dick Clough questions both the length of time taken to conclude enquiries and the consequences for staff. Account has to be taken both of the prime task of the investigation and of the interests of different interested parties.

In the next chapter I discuss the significance of the personal: the nature of looking after others, the motivation for the work and the effects on staff. Olive Stevenson raises a personal aspect of a different type. Faced with the recognition that too often residents are treated badly, any of us who are associated with residential care homes and nursing homes may feel a combination of concern, guilt and hopelessness. One alternative is what might be termed the 'realistic action' proposed by Olive Stevenson, based on a recognition that the problem is huge, that individually we cannot change the world but that it is possible, perhaps indeed an imperative, to do something.

Much of this book takes the form of a spotlight directed on the darker side of care and indeed of human nature. This does not mean that such events are typical of life in homes though, sadly, they may occur more frequently than we would wish to acknowledge. Without a recognition of the harm that occurs under a guise of 'care', attempts to construct environments that are life-enhancing, have little chance of success.

Two

The abuse of care: The person and the place

Roger Clough

INTRODUCTION

The preparation for this chapter has led me to reflect on starting my career in residential work, almost exactly thirty years ago. What was it that made me choose that particular job?

Starting from self is an integral aspect of this chapter in which I shall argue that an understanding of abuse in residential care homes and nursing homes demands an understanding of the factors that are personal as well as those that are structural and associated with institutions. Thus, in relation to the personal, I contend that we need to know something about people who abuse others in their care - and that we need to know something about ourselves.

There is a further reason for starting with the person. Residential care is concerned with the daily living arrangements for individuals: one group of people, the staff, 'look after', 'care for' or 'tend' other people, depending on the phrase used to describe the task. The 'abuse' which is the topic of this book is abuse of people, often occurring within the confines of intimate, personal care. Whatever combination of factors influence the causation of an event which ends up being categorised as abuse, typically one person abuses another.

So in this chapter I focus on people in relation to a place, the home. This is not to argue that the sort of structural factors highlighted by Evelyn McEwen or Elisabeth Henderson are not vital to an understanding of abuse. This chapter presents one dimension, while in the book as a whole we have tried to combine the personal with the structural. Understanding is limited if we distance ourselves from the debate; but our understanding is flawed also if we fail to take account of structures.

MOTIVATION

I start with a focus on the motivation of those who work in Homes. Given the emphasis I have placed on understanding self, it is useful to illustrate the general argument with examples related to our own motivation.

When asked as to why they are putting energy into work, people involved in tackling abuse might respond: 'It's an important topic' or 'We care about what happens to people'. Of course, that is right. And of course that is proper. Nevertheless, and recognising the danger of pursuing a point that some may regard as inappropriately psychoanalytic, I suggest that considering the impact of the topic on ourselves has significance.

In terms of my own background there are two significant events: being asked to write a paper for the Wagner Committee (referred to later by Frank Glendenning and Lorayne Ferguson) on what has gone wrong in establishments and heading an inspection unit in a social services department, looking at allegations and making judgements about them. But, and again I take the risk knowingly of being personal, I suspect that this is not a complete explanation of my interest and drive. Fortunately this is not the place to pursue that question. My point is that the reasons for taking up direct care work in homes and the energy that is or is not put into the job are influenced by factors such as:

- the extent to which people are interested in (even excited by) the task;
- the employment options, including conditions of service and pay;
- skills and capacity;
- the value placed by individuals on the work and the value others place on their work.

In addition, perhaps less consciously, other factors impinge, factors that are specific to experiences of caring and being cared for:

- our personal history of care and its abuse: are our experiences

good, bad or confused? are these of being cared for of caring for others?
- anxieties about self: have I the potential to neglect or harm others? do I abuse my position?

The list is intended to be illustrative and leads to the central aspect of motivation to be considered here, that of staff working in homes. The question I raised at the start of this chapter in relation to myself is relevant here to others: 'Why do people work in direct care?'. If we add a second question, 'Whose needs are being met?', one of the potential dangers in direct care is immediately exposed: it is possible that staff meet their own needs at the cost of those of the resident.

For all of us there will be a mix of motivation, attitude and behaviour in our choice of jobs and the way we carry them out. The significant aspect is that people may have what seem concerned or caring attitudes, such as 'to do good to/for others', 'to help', or 'to make happy'. However, such attitudes are not a sufficient base for good practice because, although staff may want and indeed attempt 'to do good', 'to help', 'to make happy' or whatever, they may fail to achieve their hopes. Such failure illustrates a disjunction between intent and reality.

Recent reports have emphasised the necessity for greater rigour in selection of staff. Warner (1992) makes a strong case in relation to residential work with children and young people for improvements in selection. Indeed, there are suggestions that psychological tests should be used. Yet there is an integral aspect which needs clarification before employing such tests. Do we know: what is sound motivation for the carrying out of the task? which aspects of people's interest in their job are deemed healthy or worrying? whether it matters if people are attracted by the vulnerability of others?

Thus we are confronted by huge, general questions: What attracts people to their work? What sorts of attractions are proper and what are not? One way to examine such questions is to focus on our own attractions to our work, our own feelings and uncertainties.

Moving to the specific focus on direct care, people, indeed ourselves, may like working with dependent people because:

- they believe the residents are not threatening;
- they want to be in charge;
- they get satisfaction from others' depending on them.

In particular, if staff do not feel in control in other parts of their lives; working at tending in a residential home may be satisfying and fulfilling. In itself this is neither indicative of good nor of bad outcomes for residents. Staff may give a lot and work well; but they may not. There are satisfactions to working with people who are highly dependent in parts of their lives, but there are also frustrations.

THE PRIMARY TASK IN LOOKING AFTER OTHERS

This is not the place to write at length abut the nature of the task that I and others have written about as 'residential work'. (See Clough, 1981, 1982 and 1989; Burton, 1993). But it is essential background to recall that for all staff there are traces, larger or smaller, of the following:

Aspects that are related to the 'involvement' of staff:

- exposure to the pain and hurt of residents and a seeming demand to heal and resolve;
- a wish to do something for residents, to improve their lives;
- the potential to be touched or disturbed by the experiences of residents.

Factors that are pertinent to the nature of the tasks to be undertaken, tasks that:

- may be physically demanding and unpleasant;
- having been done once will have to be done again and again for the resident who has had a bath and enjoys feeling and looking good, will get dirty and want, or need another bath;
- are carried out in public, so that how you manage is seen by other residents and staff;
- have to be completed, perhaps under pressure or at set times: meals to be cooked and washed up; residents helped with getting dressed or going to bed.

Matters that are related to helping and managing groups and individuals:

- the tension between leaving alone people who want to give up and trying to influence them;
- the expectations of others that certain types of structures will be in place, in particular that a measure of control will be exerted;
- the consequent necessity to set boundaries, to specify and

enforce requirements, all of which are aspects of power and control;
- the fact of being concerned for the welfare both of an individual resident and of other residents, between whom there may be conflicts.

Thus there are a number of reasons why staff in a residential home may find the work to be difficult, may feel that the job is out of control, may have strong feelings roused, may get hurt both physically and emotionally and may relive past experiences.

Such paid work is not the same as care by family members. Staff are free from certain of the specific tensions and responsibilities faced by informal carers, in particular by family members who care for one another: a particular responsibility, tying together emotional demands with the feeling of no escape. Nevertheless, as the earlier discussion illustrates, tending in homes is a complex and demanding task. Why then, it might be asked, do people work in nursing and residential care homes?

When I first started in residential work in 1965 there were debates as to whether people became residential workers because they wanted a measure of protection that the institution provided. At that time there seemed an underlying assumption that people who worked in residential homes were doing so for their own needs: they could not manage without the protection of the residence. There were differences from today in the work environment for many staff in residential child care and senior staff in work with adults were expected to live on the premises. Although probably at that time I would have disputed such an analysis, the reality is that, as with any job, residential workers are likely to be fulfilling their own wants and needs. At issue, and at the heart of the content of this chapter, is whether the fulfilling of personal needs is a by product of the proper undertaking of staff's work or whether the core work with residents is distorted by the way personal needs are met.

There are of course the full range of reasons for taking up residential work: job satisfaction, convenience to home, pay, job status or prospects. But there is also a specific dimension, akin to nursing, of wanting to be alongside others who are struggling to cope, perhaps in pain, despondency or despair. Staff hope perhaps to heal, certainly to comfort.

In good residential work staff not only are involved in the detail of daily life but also want to be involved in those activities. The emphasis is significant because it points to the fact that in direct care, the care is central: it is not an inconvenient extra that is slotted on to a task that is seen as oversight of people's living arrangements. The best staff will want to provide daily care. That is not to claim that staff will (or should) feel enthusiastic about all their work, but that they should enjoy looking after others.

This is similar to good parents wanting to be involved both in structuring the environment in which their children will grow up and in some parts of their daily lives. I stress that I am not arguing that residential work with adults is akin to looking after children; my point is that the most typical experience of both structuring an environment and providing direct care occurs in looking after children. It is not that older people are to be treated like children: the significant similarity is in the nature of tending. A further aspect that is, perhaps, common to all residential work is that of sharing in the lives of others, possibly sharing some of one's own.

I emphasise this aspect of residential work because I believe that one element of attraction to the job is being involved in the lives of others. This characteristic of wanting such involvement should not be seen as problematic or pathological. If the characteristic is viewed as neutral, then it becomes possible to distinguish between situations where a person wanting such involvement, (and in part being attracted to the job for this reason), is taking improper advantage of another and those occasions where the involvement not only is not taking improper advantage but is of positive benefit to the resident. It is possible also that there is a specific attraction to working with people who are vulnerable, again an attraction that should be regarded as neutral. However, this attraction also has a potential darker side, that of taking advantage of the other's vulnerability.

Many people taking up a career in various welfare activities say that they do so because of the way that they have faced and managed problems. 'I had a rough time, and got through, and want to be able to help others to do the same', typifies this approach. At the Lancaster conference, some people commented on their growing recognition of the numbers of staff in direct care who have themselves been abused. There is growing recognition also of the numbers of people in the population as a whole who have been abused. Nevertheless there may be a disproportionately high number of people working in the direct care of others who have been abused. Stone (1995) writes that:

> Nearly a quarter (22 per cent) of the 1306 randomly selected child care social workers who took part in the research say they were emotionally abused, 12 per cent

> say they were physically abused, and 11 per cent say they were subjected to sexual abuse. Four per cent say they were neglected. (p.22)

In any case, greater knowledge is needed of the implications for staff's capacity to provide direct care of having themselves been abused.

THE NATURE OF RESIDENTIAL WORK: INTIMACY, BOUNDARIES, VULNERABILITY

Residential life, by its very nature, requires that staff are involved in a number of activities which intrude into the lives of residents. The prime model on which people draw for their understanding of the task of helping with daily living and with intimate tending has been their own households and families. Our views are formed of the essentials in caring from the households in which we were children, those in which we live with other adults (in particular those who are our lovers) and those in which we look after our own children.

These have been powerful and formative: they hold memories of holding and comfort, pain and hurt; they are places in which we have blossomed and harboured resentments, been dependent and independent; in control and out of control, dependable and undependable.

Inevitably the nurturing and tending of others (whether inside or outside households) is evocative of how we have been nurtured and tended, and have ourselves nurtured and tended others. Thus the task of tending, whether as paid work or in a family, touches significant memories. The extent to which this knowledge and memory equips us for the task or reminds us of barren experiences will vary between individuals. For each individual, the capacity to work well will be influenced also by current state of well being, the particular tending tasks being undertaken or the personality and characteristics of the person for whom the care is being provided. Mike Nolan quotes Dimond's (1986) comment from a nursing assistant that the feeling towards someone affects attitude to the work to the extent of whether or not you are repelled by cleaning them: ' ... it's hard to clean somebody new, or somebody you don't like. If you like 'em, it's like your baby.'

The provision of care for adults (as opposed to children) reminds us of potential ill health, disability, old age and death, whether of ourselves or those whom we love. Tending is not an emotionally neutral activity. It has sometimes been argued that residential staff must not get emotionally involved with residents. Thus emotional distance (sometimes improperly thought of as a part of professionalism) may be striven for, in Menzies's (1960) words 'as a defence against anxiety'. Such denial of feelings does not lead to good practice. Menzies shows how attempts to keep distance result in a style of work that is destructive for both the people who are cared for and their carers. Being unwilling (or unable) to acknowledge the intensity of one's own feelings as worker does not make staff invulnerable: simply, it makes them differently vulnerable. Trying to remain emotionally detached does not lead to healthier relationships.

Thus, I argue that staff will at times find their emotions involved in the act of providing care for residents: staff will be aware of the happiness, pain or hurt of residents and they will know how the residents make them feel themselves. Staff are to be involved emotionally without being 'emotionally involved', in the way in which the words are used to describe relationships.

DIRECT CARE: THE TASK AND THE STAFF

Direct care in homes requires that staff are aware of the nature of the experience of residents because without such understanding it is too easy for the care to become routinised and insensitive. To do this staff must not remain distant and detached. A part of this insight is knowledge of what it is like to be wanting or needing others to do some looking after of oneself. Another aspect is related to the life stage of the person living in the home: what are their dreams, expectations and present reality?

In a sense, staff are to be intimate with people who do not start from being their intimates. In considering the impact of this for both resident and worker, it is worth reflecting on the different individuals we are willing to allow to do things for us. Sinclair and colleagues (1988b) catalogue the different tasks that various family members and outsiders perform. These are linked to closeness in terms of kinship and gender. The result is that close family members (and most typically sons) are expected to deal with money matters while female relatives are to provide personal care. Finch and Groves (1983) emphasise the expectations placed on women as prime carers. The only exception to this is the direct personal care between partners in old age: here, men look after women as much as women look after men. These two factors of closeness and sex of carer have significant implications for residents and workers in the provision of direct care.

This is the backcloth to worker involvement in the lives of residents. Such tending activities may be categorised in different ways:

- by the type of activity that is undertaken (for example, helping residents with getting dressed, bathing or going to the lavatory);
- as direct or indirect (helping someone to get up from a chair or keeping an eye on people to make sure that they are all right; direct physical care or cooking a meal, but not actually serving it to the resident);
- as formal or informal, alternatively structured or unstructured (the distinction here is between those activities which can be specified, such as bathing, and those that arise from spontaneous events - talking with residents who are happy or sad after receiving a letter);
- by whether the care is intimate or not (some people require help with tasks that throughout their lives they have carried out in private or with people close to them; intimacy is also about knowing of the joys and sorrows of the lives of others because their lives are more public or shared at least with some staff).

THE LINK BETWEEN PERSON AND TASK

Much of our picture of both what comprises 'care' and of how to provide it or, perhaps better, how to 'be caring', comes also from our early experiences not just in families but from friends, school, clubs and activities. It is in the same places that we have come to learn about what is and is not appropriate between the person with power (parent, teacher, other adult, carer) and the person who is dependent (child, resident). A focus on the creation of boundaries and the crossing of boundaries is useful because the horror of abuse by staff in residential and nursing care is that of being assaulted by the very people with whom one expects to be safe. In this sense such abuse has resonance to abuse by other professionals when in positions of trust: doctors, nurses, clergy, police, teachers.

POWER AND ABUSE

What is frightening about this topic is that it faces us with the reality of abuse in the very settings where we expect - and should be able to presume - on care: care in the sense not just of being looked after (having things done for me) but in the sense of being looked after in way that is caring.

And, of course, it has resonance also to abuse by parents, the people most of all whom we need and presume we can trust. We give, trust and expect security in our relationships with adult partners. We have children expecting that our homes will be places in which they will feel and be secure. To our cost we know that this does not always happen: we, or others, abuse trust; those others (or ourselves) hurt those whom once, or currently, they love. What is distinctive about an abuse of trust in a residential home is that it takes place apart from the intensity and closeness of special personal relationships.

> The woman whose 16 year old son now lives with ... his .. former teacher, is terrified by the thought of what might be going on behind the closed doors of the school. She keeps her two younger boys under surveillance for signs of exaggerated affection from teachers. 'I'm worried about them going to the school', she says. 'I've been telling them not to let anyone touch them. When your children are in school, you think they're all right. It's very worrying.' (Longrigg, 1994, p.12)

Many situations in direct care make staff aware of the parameters of their power and authority. Field social work is indirect in that staff work with people to consider how those people may act, perhaps to regain some control of their lives. Field social workers have considerable power, and have to learn what is appropriate in its management. However, staff in Homes have power of a different type related to immediate, day to day events in people's lives. These in effect are concerned with the management of others. A resident decides not to eat anything for several days: what are staff to do? Another resident who is often confused keeps walking outside the home, which worries relatives and neighbours, and confronts staff with the obvious risks: should the staff stop the person going out? Someone else does not want to go to her room but will not stop annoying a group of residents who are watching a favourite television programme? Behind any of these issues are questions as to the responsibility of different parties: residents, staff and relatives.

The examples could be multiplied endlessly, for example to include residents who are violent to other residents or staff, who demand help with activities that staff think they could do for themselves or who are dirty and smelly and will not wash or let the staff help them to wash. The issue is that the fact of living alongside others, together with the fact of needing help with certain activities, creates conflicts of interest from which staff may not just walk away. Residents have not chosen to live with particular people who are the other residents; the consequences are that many of the tensions faced in households are worked out with people with whom not only may residents not be intimate but with whom they may have nothing in common.

At the heart of the debate is the disparity in power between resident and worker. The same point is made by Longrigg (1994) about teacher-pupil relationships. 'The imbalance of power is the aspect that causes most unease ... : the teacher has an unfair advantage' (p.12).

Power differential lies at the heart of understanding abuse. Much physical abuse of residents is linked to a determination to control the actions of others whether to prevent an old person constantly repeating a plea to go home or to stop one resident behaving badly to another. Yet, the triggers to abuse are more insidious. Earlier I wrote that the seeming good intent of staff towards residents is not enough as a base for practice. This is exemplified by the staff member who wants to help someone who lives in the home and is endlessly frustrated by the resident appearing to take no account of their endeavours. Staff have the power to translate the wish to help into compelling a resident to do something that is thought to be in her or his interest. There are no easy solutions. Staff, as I have already stated, may not ignore the actions of residents, as may those of us who do not work in homes. And yet they must not abuse their power.

The staff member who abuses another imposes their interpretation on the other person. Frequently, abusers justify their actions by claiming either that their intent was good or that their acts did no harm to the other. 'I like (or love) the people for whom I care: how could it be thought that I would harm them?', runs the defence. The essential starting point, as Olive Stevenson argues in the final chapter, is that abuse must be stopped, whatever action is taken towards the staff member. Understanding the causation of abuse must not result in a toleration of abuse.

The consequence of my argument is that all parties (residents, relatives, staff, management, advocates and public) must have an understanding of the rights and responsibilities of residents and staff. The power that exists in relation to the minute details of daily life must be explicit and must be managed.

Some forms of physical, emotional and sexual abuse may have a common factor in the satisfaction derived from the wielding of power over another person. In Homes, frequently this is compounded by the defenceless state of the resident.

There is abundant evidence that residents feel powerless. This develops from the residents' basic position of needing help with tasks which others manage for themselves (and indeed not being able to live satisfactorily without such help). The manner in which staff assist residents may compound or minimise such feelings of dependence and powerlessness. Thus, the residential home does not create the fact that residents are not in control of certain aspects of their lives: but it may make residents feel more or less in control. Power is demonstrated not just in formal ways but in the subtleties of daily interaction: a resident asks a staff member for assistance; the staff member says that she/he will come back later, but fails to do so; the resident is left waiting and not knowing if the staff member is going to return. (See Clough, 1981, pp. 82-94 and 157-65).

The factor that distinguishes the staff member who abuses residents from one who does not is not that the abuser necessarily is attracted to the work by different factors than the non abuser: rather it is that the abuser fails to set limits to personal behaviour which ensure that the interests, needs or satisfaction of the staff member do not become paramount over that of the resident.

Power is connected also with relationships between people. Once again staff need to be aware of their power in relation to residents, the dependence of residents and the significance of interaction to residents. Residents live alongside others and witness the intimacies of their lives, contacts which may lead to friendships and fantasies. Some will see their life in the home as a result of a lack of loving relationships: 'If my children loved me more ...' or 'If I could find someone to love me ...perhaps I would not have to live here'. (See Clough, 1981, pp. 119 and 178). The 'escape from the present' takes the form for some people of dreams of love.

However, as Townsend (1962) showed a long time ago, living alongside people whom one has not chosen does not make it likely that people will make friends. Surprisingly few residents described close relationships with other residents. In homes residents are likely to have close physical proximity to others and to be aware of intimate situations in their lives: getting up and going to bed, going to the toilet, having a bath. Mostly this will be knowledge of what is happening in the lives of others but at times there will be glimpses of these scenes: people in dressing gowns or the doors of bedrooms or bathrooms left open. Sexual fantasies may exist.

This background is important as the context in which staff work with residents. The fantasies or interest may be those of residents or staff. Given that the task of caring for other people is acknowledged to be both necessary and important, what is to be regarded as 'proper' or healthy' in the way in which staff bath residents? We want people to be cared for and indeed, perhaps, to feel cherished. But we do not expect bath times to be occasions for the excitement or gratification of staff or residents. How are staff to wash and dry someone, being caring and not over interested?

When a situation occurs to which the term 'abuse' properly is applied, there has been the transgression of a boundary of acceptable behaviour. There may have been earlier stages in the actions of the staff member or resident when the boundary between acceptable and unacceptable was not so well defined. For example it may be difficult for all parties to work out whether the way someone is held is or is not an abuse. People may be held to comfort, to physically support or to prevent them harming themselves or others. The example is useful because it illustrates both the complexity in setting boundaries and the way in which the physical tending of residents may be turned into acts of physical or sexual assault: comforting someone may turn to fondling; stopping someone from doing something may turn into physical cruelty.

We have to accept that there is difficulty in defining the boundary and, that views of acceptability will differ. Yet it is helpful also to focus on events which would be widely accepted as abuse. There is something significant about crossing a clear boundary of this type. In effect what has happened is that a taboo has been overridden. Once that has happened, it becomes progressively easier to override the taboo and to stay in the previously forbidden territory for longer periods. This can be seen as learned behaviour.

At first glance it may seem extraordinary, even inconceivable, that people who are themselves highly dependent or defenceless are assaulted by others. Sadly, there is increasing evidence of the extent to which children are abused within families. There are sharp distinctions between life in households and direct care work in particular that in direct care the carers have chosen to work, in a particular job and have been employed for that task, unless they are owners of the facility. Nevertheless there are aspects of similarity, such as the transgression of what has been thought a safe boundary.

The trigger for abuse may be factors such as:

- the various frustrations of the work (too much to do in too little time; the impossible to relieve unhappiness of residents); *or*
- the attempt to manage problematic behaviour.

In relation to staff who abuse residents, there may be a temptation to see some as people who are after their own gratification and others who are frustrated by aspects of the task of caring. The reality is more complex: those who are frustrated may in part be frustrated that they cannot control others, as well as that they cannot control the task; those who are thought to want gratification may in many ways be good workers, providing sensitive care. Thus, satisfaction for self and concern for others are intertwined for all direct care workers.

Workers who tend others have to ensure that they construct boundaries and taboos that recognise the worker's feelings and involvement when tending others. Thus we face one of the underlying themes of abuse in residential homes: are those who abuse others drawn into the work because, knowingly or not, it provides an opportunity for them to abuse others? Alternatively, do people enter the work and find themselves in situations where they cannot or will not restrain their actions? Further, do the same factors apply to those who neglect, physically abuse or sexually abuse others?

The welfare of children in effect is to be safeguarded by the establishment of boundaries and taboos. The boundaries are constructed so that, for example, we know the limits to tickling and play. Parents (as well as other relatives) may well be attracted by their children, revelling in physical play, knowing that they as well as the child enjoy the activities and, indeed, that they enjoy the physical proximity and intimacy. The construction of boundaries may well not be conscious, but factors related to our own sexual arousal or that of our children are significant indicators in establishing boundaries. There may be occasions when, given thought, adults may become uneasy as to what is proper. A recent report on prison staff working with serious sex offenders, included a reference to a male prison officer who had decided not to bath his two young boys of 7 and 9, because of his anxiety about what is proper behaviour. (BBC, 1995)

Boundaries have to be established also in residential work because 'Staff must be involved in the same intimate events (as parents) without the assurance which parents have that such intimate involvement is acceptable in society.' (Clough, 1982, p.130). The recognition of abuse by staff is leading to changed behaviour of staff. In residential child care, staff are much less likely to touch or hold children and young people. Some agencies, in response to management (and public) anxiety, have produced guidelines which demonstrate the extremes of defensiveness which lead to a terrible travesty of 'care' or tending: thus, in day nurseries, one authority requires that two staff must be present when babies and young children are having nappies changed. The waves from discoveries of abuse extend in ever wider circles: we no longer know on what or whom we can rely.

ABUSE BY CARERS

The patterns that lead to abuse in residential care of older people are not the same as those in households. Nor is all abuse in residential care triggered by the same events. Authors in this book such as Frank Glendenning and Mike Nolan suggest that the evidence is limited on the total volume of abuse and the amount of different types of abuse. There are suggestions that the most frequent sort of abuse of residents is emotional, followed by physical and sexual. (I am excluding 'financial abuse' from this discussion, as explained earlier). 'Emotional abuse' is used to cover neglect, in the sense of ignoring people and cruelty, including verbal attacks. The motivation for such abuse, and the environmental and structural factors which create or perpetuate it, are very different from those related to physical or sexual assaults. If there is to be appropriate action on abuse, it is imperative to start with escaping from a notion of a coherent whole termed 'abuse'.

Some factors are known about who commits abuse. Ann Craft shows that as in abuse of children, men are the overwhelming majority of abusers of adults with learning disabilites. (p.73) However, I think that in the direct care of older people, the pattern may differ: while there are only a very few women who sexually abuse older people, there may be a significant proportion who physically abuse or emotionally neglect others. This is a prime area for research so that actions are based on knowledge.

In summary, the characteristics of abuse by staff in residential homes are that:

- people who as staff are trusted by residents, relatives and the public to look after others demonstrate their untrustworthiness;
- people with power over others use it improperly to control or humiliate; such power may be of physical strength but arises also from being a provider of services to people who are dependent for physical care and who may well be little able to complain or take their trade elsewhere;
- in doing so staff are likely to be satisfying their own needs;
- staff know of the vulnerabilities of residents;
- staff may be involved in the intimate physical care of others;
- the secrecy required of perpetrator and victim has parallels with that within families in terms of systems to maintain that secrecy.

ABUSE BY RESIDENTS

The recognition of the power which staff hold and exercise over residents may blind us to seeing the power that residents hold over one another and staff. Olive Stevenson cites what she terms 'the naked power' of one resident controlling the lives of others. The investigation which led to the drive to hold the conference was of an elderly male resident assaulting numbers of female residents over a period of several years. Residents have and use power in relation to their own lives: they determine whether or not to do certain things and it is probable that when there is minimal opportunity for control over much of one's own life, some residents exercise determined control over aspects of their behaviour. Others physically assault residents or staff. Once again we are faced with a need to recognise that an understanding of the reasons for such behaviour must not result in acceptance of it.

Abuse by residents does not figure largely in this book. There are fewer statistics as to its extent and less focus in discussions. In part this stems from the fact that residents are the clients and staff may think that they have to be tolerant of their behaviour. The reader needs to bear this in mind in considering abuse in homes.

PERSONAL REFLECTION

It is inevitable and proper that allegations of abuse arouse strong feelings. Such feelings must be recognised so that the work is managed appropriately and not driven by emotions which are not acknowledged. There are a number of dimensions to such self awareness. The first relates to questions about one's own capacity to abuse others:

> Have I ever done things which have any similarity with the events about which disgust is being registered?
>
> Have I ever ... lost control, hit someone, forced another person to do what I wanted them to do, abused power?

The second dimension is a search for understanding of the situations in which one is more likely to lose control or abuse power. As I muse on myself in residential work, I think of the occasions when I lost my temper, the situations in which then or now I am aware of my vulnerability and the potential in me to take advantage of others.

Thirdly, there is the set of feelings concerned with the reaction to the event: what does the allegation make me feel and think? I think it important to be aware of the mix, indeed ambivalence in reaction: perhaps, anger and distrust but also an interest in trying to understand and imagine what the events are like for different parties, an element possibly, of voyeurism.

Finally, there are the feelings related to the role in which one hears about the allegation, as manager, colleague, someone working for the same authority or as investigator.

And I know too of the powerful memories from my own residential work. The episodes were significant because they relate to the deep feelings and concerns of living. Residential life is not only necessary but important for many people. We must aim for residents to feel safe, for staff to know how vital that is for dependent people - and for everyone to know what to do if they have concerns.

Three

Abuse in residential care: Reflections from the mid-Atlantic

Annie Zlotnick

As I recall 1977 was our annus horribilis in New York City. Scandal after scandal of elder abuse in residential care made front page news. All forms of elder abuse were very much in evidence There were reports of fraudulent claims on pension cheques by nursing home owners long after the recipients had died. Testimony of family, friends and residents bearing witness to physical abuse and neglect became standard.

How did it happen? We wondered, we who worked in residential care. The answer to that question was debated by residents, families, friends, staff, government and the news media for the days, months and years to follow. My recollections are that explanations in the press centred around the large number of elderly people without families falling prey to private nursing home operators, as most, if not all of the homes about which complaints were made were in the private sector. (The term 'nursing home' was used generically to refer to all old people's homes) . The large number of homes opening quickly to accommodate a burgeoning population of over 65s led to a situation which was insufficiently regulated to ensure standards of quality care.

Explanations that satisfied staff were much harder to come by. As a social worker in a large residential home, my role was to provide social services and counselling services for residents and family members. My staff and I arranged for pre-admission tours and discussions, assisted in the actual admission and were responsible for the ongoing social aspects of the care plans which were also worked on by nursing and medical staff. One day I arrived at work to see my boss being arrested for financial irregularities. (Later we discovered that he had submitted inflated bills for services). We were shocked and horrified that our gentle director, who regularly talked with the residents and had always acted as their advocate, could have been involved.

It was a difficult time; all members of staff shared the mantle of guilt, even if we did not deserve it. Everyone who worked in residential care was a marked person who was seen as cruel and exploitative. I remember constantly feeling as if I had to defend my decision to work in residential care. This coupled with the perceived low status accorded social workers was indeed a double indemnity. Fellow staff from all disciplines did share the feeling that we were being attacked in the media and perhaps by the public at large. We also felt that those individuals who opted for residential care were being judged alongside their families. Anecdotal material about happy residents in homes was scarce.

Now 18 years later I am living in the UK (where I have been for the past 7 years). The Lancaster conference has led me to reflect on my experiences of so long ago. Since my arrival in the UK I have been working as a training consultant in the areas of abuse, community care and management development. These experiences have given me the opportunity to re-think many of the issues that were raised as far back as 1977. They are still relevant today in 1995.

In New York the issues of abuse were first uncovered within the residential care and nursing homes sector whereas in the UK, raised awareness about abuse seems to have begun in the community - in the family, inside people's private homes. From my recent experiences in working with abuse in the UK , I began to realise that there is a fundamental difference in attitude towards the treatment of abuse by virtue of where it takes place. This difference also affects one's thinking around the issues of abuse. Residents in care were seen by those of us working in New York in 1977 as vulnerable people who had been placed in our care because they were disabled in some way. Many were elderly people who had been institutionalised in the mental health system for so long that they were terrified of living outside of the residential setting. In addition to their physical and mental infirmities some were victims of crime, poor housing and deteriorating inner city neighbourhoods where they were prisoners in their own homes. We felt we had to protect them. This view also took into account the rights of the residents to their own lives and to take their own decisions together with their right to be safe.

In the UK, when participating in discussion and case conferences on the best way to handle abuse in the community, I hear great debates raging over the rights of residents to stay in abusive environments surrounded by abusive family members. As practitioners, carers and social workers we are there as an agency, to offer help in the form of services or alternatives to the abusive lifestyle. We cannot force the abused individuals to take advantage of our services. This raises difficult questions and is a real challenge to our systems and policies especially when those involved are suffering from increasing dementia and cannot express their views.

How is this rather admirable respect for individual human rights interpreted when it comes to those in residential care and not in the community? Do we allow residents to stay in residential care if they choose to do so despite practices which border on neglect and abuse? Could residents insist on staying in an abusive residential home because they see this as 'home'? Does this apply to all homes - run by local authorities, health authorities or privately run homes? Is there a distinction in the right to protection for those who choose to go into residential care as opposed to those who are in their own homes?

So far in the UK, the focus for setting up abuse protection policies has been in the community. Now there is a stronger need to define these policies for residential care establishments. How was the situation resolved in New York? A set of standards for homes was set up with a strict enforcement mechanism. Homes could be inspected by a multidisciplinary team any time of the day or night. Formal inspections were held unannounced at least once a year. Stiff penalties were imposed if homes did not measure up to standards and a substantial number of homes were closed down.

In addition a complaints mechanism was set up. Complaints of lack of care or abuse could be reported anonymously twenty four hours a day to a central number which logged the complaints and had to act upon them in twenty four hours. Formal staff , i.e. those who were working in residential homes and especially those with licences to practise (doctors, social workers etc.) were under legal obligation to report any and all abuse or risk losing their licences to practice. We found this practice to be helpful in that we had to report abuse and wasted no time on debating the issue of reporting. We were also assured of an outside agency investigating the abuse and lessening the opportunity for cover-ups. Some of the complaints were calls from lonely residents who wanted to speak to someone. Other reported cases were serious including the rape of a resident by another resident.

In looking back, I do remember this all being a very difficult time. At first staff morale was badly bruised by the imposition of inspections and unannounced visits.

The complaints from residents and families increased now that they had a safe forum for these complaints within a legal framework. Staff felt scrutinised and there was the odd grumble that there should be a mechanism to complain about the residents who could also be abusive both verbally and physically.

However, the implementation of standards did serve to raise morale over time. It created a sense of achievement, with clear goals and standards of care which had to be achieved. I can honestly say that when I returned to the same home as manager a few years later, I was able to work with staff to ensure a very high standard including the attainment of an exceptional rating on the inspection survey. After announcing the results of the survey, I was delighted to find that the morale among residents, families and staff was much raised and a far cry from the low ebb of the scandals. This experience once again stressed for me the need to consider staff when it comes to allegations of abuse. It was reassuring for staff to work towards publicly accepted standards and prove themselves to be the true professionals that they were striving to be. I could not believe that this was the same home that had been so low just a few years ago. The delight and camaraderie among residents, staff, family and the community was the highlight of my career.

What did I learn from my experiences now reviewed through a looking glass of almost twenty years of experience?

The importance of establishing clearly defined roles for both management and staff. These roles should best be defined by residents, staff and management in an open forum so that expectations can also be examined. *Home Life* or *Homes are for Living* in could be used as a basis for these discussions. Defining roles would also create the opportunity to discuss situations that may be deemed abusive by one group and not by another. Roles imply both rights and responsibilities on the part of all involved-residents, staff, families and management. An abusive climate can be created between management and staff or staff and families and then spill over to residents.

Complaints systems are now part of the caring environment. How effective are they and how do we measure their effectiveness? How can these systems be responsive to staff as well as to residents, families and friends. A complaint must be viewed as an opportunity for improvement not a signal for blame. In this regard I do wish that our system in New York had focused more on strategies for the prevention and reoccurrence of abuse rather than just the investigation into a particular incident.

Discussions at Lancaster have revived my thinking on these topics. The disparate views expressed by an entire group committed to eradicating abuse from the residential scene served to remind me of the great need for dialogue amongst all involved. If this dialogue has begun in earnest in Lancaster, then long may it continue!

Part Two:

The Background to Abuse: Prevalence and Characteristics

Four

The mistreatment of elderly people in residential institutions

Frank Glendenning

The mistreatment of elderly people in care homes and hospitals is never far from headlines in the press. So it is singular that we have been slow in Britain to find out what we can learn from bringing together the American findings and setting them alongside the considerable evidence that we have in this country from the reports of official enquiries into the mistreatment of elderly people in care homes.

Phillipson and Biggs suggested recently that because the dominant approach in the research literature has been to apply the family violence model, this has tended to underplay concern in residential settings. So whilst the extent of abuse in informal or family settings is very unclear, its existence within institutions in Britain has been widely documented (Phillipson and Biggs, 1995: 189). Townsend published The Last Refuge in 1962 (in which he described the gradual process of depersonalisation which overtook elderly people in residential care) and since then there have been reports by: Robb on hospitals in 1967; Willcocks, Peace and Kellaher on residential homes in the public sector in 1986; Roger Clough's hitherto unpublished overview of official enquiry reports, Scandals in Residential Centres, which was prepared at the request of the Wagner Committee in 1988; Holmes and Johnson on private homes in 1988; Horrock's analysis of Health Advisory Service reports (cited in Tomlin, 1989: 11); the Harman sisters' report on the first 96 cases considered under the

1984 Registered Homes Act in 1989; and Counsel and Care's reports on privacy and restraint in 1991 and 1992.

When discussing this subject it has been customary to draw a distinction between individual acts of abuse in institutions and actual institutional or institutionalised abuse. As Decalmer has suggested (Decalmer and Glendenning, 1993: 59) abuse of the person is common, but the commonest abuse of all is institutional abuse, where the environment, practices and rules of the institution become abusive in themselves. Bennett and Kingston have argued that there is a deficiency in research that could be used to explain and remedy the socialisation processes that lead to abusing behaviour in institutions (Bennett and Kingston, 1993: 116). Higgs and Victor have also reminded us that there are few longitudinal studies which enable us to examine the influence of age, or indeed other variables, like health status and availability of family care, on the probability of moving into institutional care (Higgs and Victor, 1993: 193). These comments are all important.

One commentator wrote in the *Nursing Times* at the time of the Nye Bevan Lodge scandal in 1987:

> It is self-evident that when elderly, often confused residents are made to eat their own faeces, are left unattended, are physically manhandled or are forced to pay money to care staff and even helped to die, there is something seriously wrong (Vousden, 1987:19).

And Callahan asking questions about the American definitions of elder abuse said in 1988:

> What difference does it make, after all, whether an older person is hit or ignored, wilfully hurt or unwittingly neglected, financially exploited or psychologically attacked? Something needs to be done (Callahan, 1988: 453).

Phillipson has suggested that it is invidious to select any one setting for particular emphasis and that we should look for an approach which sees abuse as an issue which is not tied to any one context or relationship (Phillipson 1993:84). Nevertheless the evidence of abusive behaviour in residential settings is well documented in this country. The issue is how, with our existing knowledge, should we proceed in relation to our understanding of elder abuse and our search for strategies to prevent it?

It is necessary to place the discussion into some kind of

context, without going back to demographic issues. Higgs and Victor show that between 1970 and 1990 the number of residential places nearly doubled, reaching nearly half a million places, over 200,000 being in the independent sector. They trace the increase to the rapid growth of private residential and nursing home places during the 1980s resulting from a change in the Supplementary Benefit (SB) regulations. The regulations now enabled older people with low incomes to enter care at no cost to themselves. In 1980, local SB offices were given discretion under Rule 9 to enable them to pay board and lodging allowances to older people in private homes at rates which were 'reasonable'. This doubled the number of claimants between 1980 and 1983 and raised annual expenditure from £18 million to £102 million. By 1990, this had reached £5.5 billion (Higgs and Victor, 1993: 190). This unexpected growth in expenditure is the total antithesis of the policy objective of community care and led the Audit Commission's report in 1986 to argue that this was a 'perverse' incentive favouring institutionalisation rather than community care (see Parker, 1990; Higgs and Victor, 1993). This provided the stimulus for the Griffiths Report and the 1990 NHS and Community Care Act.

But with growth there had also been problems in standards of care. The Harmans in 1989 found 'evidence of abuse, binding residents with cord, misuse of drugs, fraud, fire hazard, lack of hygiene and a sorry tale of bruised and miserable residents'. They also found that the Registered Homes Act 1984 was not as detailed and as clearly drafted as it might have been and had not given the registration authorities or the Tribunal wide enough powers to protect residents in homes (Harman and Harman, 1989: 4), a view shared by Brammer in her more recent paper (Brammer, 1994: 436). All this is by way of preliminary comment.

I intend first to summarise briefly the findings of various small-scale American studies and then to deal with Pillemer and Moore's study in 1989 in more detail because their significant report has not been widely available in Britain.

Twenty years ago, May Sarton the American novelist, who died, at the age of 83, as I was writing this paper, published a novel called *As We Are Now* about the experiences of her principal character, Caro, in a private residential home. She identified in the novel various types of abuse numbers of years before the researchers caught up with the issue. It is however coincidental that in the same year that the novel was published, Stannard published a paper in America in *Social Problems* entitled 'Old folks and dirty work' based on his participant observation study of a nursing home where he identified slapping, hitting, shaking a patient, pulling hair, tightening restraining belts and terrorising by gesture or word (Stannard, 1973).

Kimsey, Tarbox and Bragg in 1981 examined 1,000 nursing homes in Texas and wrote:

> Deliberate physical abuse by formal caretakers was less common. Physical neglect was far more common, for example the development of bedsores, inadequate nutrition, improper medication and vermin infestation. Psychological abuse was most frequent in the area of passive neglect with patients regarded as 'going to die anyway', (cited in Hudson, 1988: 22).

Kimsey built up a profile of the total nursing home population in Texas of 77,000 as being: average age 82; 95 per cent over 65 and 70 per cent over 79; the ratio of women was 2:1; most patients were poor and isolated; more than 50 per cent had some mental impairment; half had no close relatives; and fewer than 50 per cent could walk alone.

Tarbox followed this report with a paper in 1983 on the psychological aspects of neglect in nursing homes, in which he emphasised the lack of cleanliness and attractiveness in the physical environment, inadequate diet, lack of attention to the grooming of patients, infantilisation and passive neglect (Tarbox, 1983: 29-52).

Doty and Sullivan in 1983 reported on their study of statistics from the Federal Certification Agency. Out of a sample of 550 skilled nursing facilities nation-wide with 54,000 beds, as of September 1980, seven per cent of facilities were cited by the Agency as:

> deficient on the requirement that patients' rights, policies and procedures ensure that each patient admitted to the facility is free from mental and physical abuse and free from chemical and (except in an emergency) physical restraints except as authorised by the physician. (cited in Hudson, 1988: 21).

Their study showed that a significant proportion were assessed as 'deficient on the requirement that each patient is treated with consideration, respect and full dignity', fifteen per cent fitting this category in eight specific states and seven per cent nation-wide. (Pillemer and Moore, 1990: 11).

They also reported from their study of New York City nursing homes that there was evidence of over-medication and unsanitary conditions and that patients who were unable to feed themselves were not being fed. Further they contended:

> it is not uncommon for problems of patient abuse, neglect and mistreatment in nursing homes to be dismissed on the grounds that the evidence is anecdotal. The implication is that a journalist or politician 'on the make' can always go out and uncover a horror story or two (cited in Hudson, 1988:21).

In 1980, over 3,000 cases of potential Medicaid fraud were being investigated in different states and Halamandaris who was a senior lawyer at the time published a paper in 1983, which listed a cavalcade of abuse in American nursing homes: theft from patients' funds, false claims by carers to Medicare and Medicaid, trading in real estate, fraudulent therapy and pharmaceutical charges, even involvement in organised crime (Halamandaris 1983:104-14).

Stathopoulos reported in 1983 on the fact that a consumer advocacy organisation (Consumer Advocates for Better Care) had to develop strategies in nursing homes in North Central Massachusetts to deal with financial abuse, denial of civil rights, removal from private or semi-private rooms to three- or four-bedroom wards, neglect, psychological abuse and various kinds of maltreatment (Stathopoulos, 1983:336-54). The organisation developed strategies in the following way.

The foremost goal was to improve the quality of care in nursing homes and to alter the power equilibrium in favour of the consumers. The Advocates focused on local, rather than on state, nursing homes. The organisation sought funding on the understanding that it would have programme independence. It emphasised the importance of providing training for volunteer advocates and the importance of networking. At the end of the exercise, Stathopoulos reflected that 'elder abuse in institutions is one part of the continuum of abuse in our society. Public policy which supports institutionalisation of the elderly to the exclusion of other forms of care in the community is in many instances the root of elder abuse in institutions' (Stathopoulos, 1983:353).

Then Solomon investigated the pharmacological and non-pharmacological abuse of elderly patients by health care professionals and concluded that:

> poorly trained caretakers can command lesser pay but have an extremely high turnover rate ... The frustrations of the job and the debility of the patients promote infantilisation, derogation and actual physical abuse (Solomon, 1983: 159).

In 1982, in Canada, Goldstein and Blank in an editorial for the Canadian Medical Association Journal addressed the question of elder abuse in what the Schlesingers described as a 'biased and over-simplistic way' (Schlesinger and Schlesinger, 1988: 143). It caused some furore, especially as the editors alluded to alleged abuse in Canadian residential institutions without presenting any data. Further, in an attempt to exonerate the institutions, they stated that staff in residential homes were often scapegoated by patients and their relatives, leaving caregivers unable to reply. Subsequently the matter re-emerged in 1985 when the *Toronto Star* responded to a statement from the Ontario Nursing Homes' Association that 'the picture of nursing homes as substandard, uncaring institutions is false'. As Doty and Sullivan had warned might happen in 1983, the paper despatched a reporter to visit 14 homes in the Toronto area; he claimed that he found evidence which supported complaints that had been received by a task force funded by the Medical Association. These complaints had received media attention and not surprisingly the Ontario Nursing Homes' Association had objected. The reporter observed or was told of physical and material abuse, multiple instances of psychological abuse, poor nursing care, neglect, lack of attention to patients' grooming and hygiene, falsification of patients' charts, improper physical restraints and doctors' instructions being ignored (Hudson, 1988: 21-2). Although anecdotal, this episode is not without significance.

Finally in 1990, Fader published a paper in the Clinical Gerontologist on a study of health care workers in long-term care settings in New York and the way in which they perceived elder abuse in relation to active and passive neglect. By using the student T-test, nurse aides were found to have significantly lower scores than licensed practical nurses and other groups when taken together. Questions relating to passive neglect were frequently answered incorrectly by all groups. The researchers' conclusion was that there must be ongoing education and training about abuse and neglect (Fader et al., 1990; see also Foner, 1994).

Thus, there was no lack of awareness among North American investigators about the existence of the problem in the 1980s. But apart from the Texas study, not until 1989 did we have a thorough review of abuse in nursing homes by Pillemer and Moore (1989, 1990), which Pillemer revisited with Lachs in 1995. Although mentioned briefly by McCreadie in her study of abuse in domestic settings in 1991, their findings were not widely accessible in Britain until Bennett and Kingston obtained permission to publish them in 1993; their conclusion was that when Pillemer and Moore's evidence is set alongside the evidence of the British official enquiry reports, it may be that, as Pillemer has indicated, abuse in institutions is relatively widespread (Bennett and Kingston, 1993: 126).

Pillemer and Moore, in attempting to establish the prevalence of elder abuse in nursing homes, came to the conclusion that the figures provided so far were likely to be underestimates of the actual incidence of maltreatment and that official statistics merely scratched the surface of the problem. They refer to Monk's survey in 1984 which found that over half the nursing home residents in the sample had refrained from making a complaint at one time or another, because they were fearful of reprisals if they complained to a nursing home ombudsman or other state official. In drawing a distinction between 'proprietary' and 'non-profit' homes, Monk also found that there was less fear of reprisals in the latter (Pillemer, 1988: 232).

So Pillemer and Moore conducted a random-sample survey of nursing home staff in one state. Fifty-seven nursing homes were invited to participate and the final sample was drawn from 32 homes, which ranged in size from 19 to 300 beds. This yielded a sample of 577 nurses and nursing aides and telephone interviews were conducted in Spring 1987.

Pillemer and Moore recognised that it was critical to examine the issue of the extent of abuse and the causes of maltreatment within the general context of nursing home care. They built up a profile of staff and, recognising the wide range of settings that exists, confined their investigation to skilled nursing facilities, which provided 24-hour care, and to intermediate care nursing homes where intensive care was not required but where the patients had functional impairments. 'Staff' were defined as registered nurses, licensed practical nurses and nursing aides. The profile showed that the average length of employment was under five years and the average length of total employment was 7 years. Ages ranged from 16 to 64, with an average age of 40.

The data presented a picture of staff who were motivated by a desire to help others and to have meaningful employment. Staff believed that they were in an occupation that was recognised and accepted. Seventy-nine per cent felt that they had at least some authority in determining what tasks to perform and ninety-one per cent felt that they had some authority in setting the pace of their work. Thirty-two per cent found the job very stressful; forty four per cent moderately so; fifteen per cent a little stressful; ten per cent not at all. Although comparable data for other occupations were not available, these seemed to Pillemer and Moore to be high levels of job stress.

Lack of time was given as one reason for stress. The more personalised tasks like walking, talking and helping residents with personal care activities were identified as the ones not done. Forty-three per cent reported that fewer staff turned up than were scheduled on their shift on three or more days a week. Many reported high levels of burnout, based on results obtained from responses to a burnout inventory developed for human services workers (Maslach, 1982). Similarly, fifty-seven per cent agreed that they sometimes treated patients more impersonally than they would like and thirty-seven per cent said that the job hardened them emotionally. When all these data were collated, thirty-two per cent were classified as being in the 'high burnout' category and the study went on to show that burnout was strongly related to stress and therefore ways of reducing stress was a major priority for administrators. Training needs were seen to be critical for the management of patient behaviour and aggression.

Thirty-six per cent of the sample had seen at least one incident of physical abuse during the preceding year. Seventy per cent had seen staff yelling at patients. Fifty per cent had seen staff insult or swear at patients during the preceding year. The majority said that such actions had occurred more than once. Ten per cent admitted that they themselves had committed such actions. Six per cent had used excessive restraint. Forty per cent had committed at least one act of psychological abuse during the preceding year. Denying food or privileges was reported by thirteen per cent. Pillemer and Moore suggest that, as the survey was based on self-reporting, some under-reporting of negative actions had probably occurred (Pillemer and Moore, 1989:318).These estimates, they admit, cannot be compared with other estimates, which do not exist in a compatible form. But there is sufficiently extensive evidence of abuse to merit concern.

Separate statistical analyses were made to identify predictors of negative actions, paying attention to staff-patient conflict and level of burnout.

Pillemer developed his work on predictors in a paper with Bachman-Prehn in 1991. That study concludes that well-qualified staff do not choose to work in nursing homes. Work in nursing homes is physically taxing, wages are poor and job prestige is low (Pillemer, 1988: 232). Working in situations of very high conflict, staff also run serious risk of verbal and physical assault by patients. This point is reiterated in the findings of a study in Bristol and published in the *British Medical Journal* in 1993 (Eastley, MacPherson, Richards and Mian, *BMJ*, 1993 307: 845). Pillemer also drew attention to the quality of care in nursing homes which had been shown to be better in homes which could afford to hire staff with better training and where staff-patient ratios were relatively high. High staff turnover rates could be correlated with poor quality care. Nurses and nursing aides with lower levels of education and younger staff members were likely to have more negative attitudes towards elderly people (Pillemer, 1988: 232).

The outcome of this survey was an endeavour to improve staff training. Together with Hudson and others, Pillemer developed a model abuse prevention programme for nursing assistants called *Ensuring An Abuse-Free Environment* (Carie, 1991; Pillemer and Hudson, 1993). In so doing they underscored the necessity of upgrading the quality of nursing home care. In brief, the model programme is made up of eight modules written in non-technical language and includes a module on the abuse of staff by residents.

Finally, Pillemer and Moore emphasised that inappropriate management practices and staff-patient interaction require further study. Staff shortages may be a factor in inadequate care. Staff screening and development are needed to protect patients and steps must be taken to reduce the stress experienced by staff.

Wiener and Kayser-Jones published a paper in 1990 about the interaction between nursing home staff and patients and their relatives. They showed that both staff and patients/relatives had complaints of the other: the staff complained largely of being short-staffed and the sense that they were not working as a team, with restrictions placed on them by a lack of resources and actual materials to do the job, such as sheets, towels and simple ointments (Wiener and Kayser-Jones 1990: 95; cf. Kayser-Jones, 1990; see also Tellis-Nayak, 1989).

Goffman said thirty years ago:

> Many institutions, most of the time, seem to function merely as storage dumps for inmates, but they usually present themselves to the public as rational organisations designed consciously as effective machines for producing a few officially avowed and officially approved ends (Goffman, 1968: 73).

Turning from the United States to Britain, in 1981 Clough published *Old Age Homes* and emphasised the rights and choices to which residents were entitled. Urging that they should achieve some degree of 'mastery' or self-determination, he said: 'The more services the staff provide, or the more they do for residents, the more power they have over their lives' (Clough, 1981: 162), thus drawing attention to the danger that is implicit in inhibiting personal growth by restricting freedom and movement. Since then, Clough has continually drawn attention to the quality of care in residential homes. In 1988, the Wagner Committee received his report *Scandals in Residential Centres*. This was an analysis of the reports of some twenty official enquiries and raised fundamental questions about the nature of residential institutions. He reflected on what we had not learnt from the past and noted the published statement of a former Secretary for Social Services, in 1979:

> We have had a succession of public enquiries pointing up grave inadequacies in public hospitals ... [but] little has changed for the better in some [of them] ... I am determined that this gap between the good and the bad shall not remain as wide as it is today (cited in Clough, 1988).

Clough then set the scene by going back to this example written in 1955:

> John had been lying in a urine soaked bed.
> Then the nurse came. He pulled back the three blankets which covered John and said 'You filthy bastard'. He took hold of the nightshirt. John took hold of the nightshirt. They tugged. John held on as if the split shirt was life. The nurse swore. John swore. The nurse lifted a closed fist and crashed it into John's stomach. John let go. The nurse changed John's nightshirt. John's nightshirt was changed several times before he died the next day.
> He was sixty-three.

It was a chronics' ward.
It was a mental hospital.
It was a progressive hospital.
It was the twentieth century.
It was 1955. (cited in Clough, 1988)

Clough went on to comment on this example of abuse and the others that were to follow in his report saying: 'Even [these examples] cannot convey what it must have been like for dependent, powerless people to live in fear of those who had the responsibility to look after them, *day after day after day*'.

In spite of the strength of the Minister's words in 1979, by 1987 there were at least two more public enquiries. One was a report illustrating the poor management of care homes for older people in Camden and there was the appalling report about pervasive abuse at Nye Bevan Lodge, Southwark. Even more reports were to follow. Wardhaugh and Wilding in their recent paper on the corruption of care, said of one scandal:

What is remarkable is that every level of management appears to have been guilty. Middle and senior management were equally contemptuous of complaints and dilatory in pursuing them. So were Hospital Management Committees, Regional Hospital Boards and the Department of Health and Social Security. As [Dick] Crossman's memoirs reveal (Political diaries Vol.3. 411), the Department knew about the unsatisfactory conditions at Ely Hospital [Cardiff] long before the Howe Report (Whardaugh and Wilding, 1993: 18-19).

The Camden report followed complaints about the standard of care in homes for older people in the Borough. It revealed that the standard of care was poor in the majority of homes and concluded that 'effective management of residential care in Camden has broken down' (cited in Clough, 1988). This was only eight years ago.

The same year to make matters worse, there was the Nye Bevan Lodge enquiry. The report stated that there was:

> an atmosphere of deep mistrust and suspicion which [had] permeated every aspect of life in the home for many years resulting in a serious deterioration in the level of care provided [and] was such that a proper level of caring could never be restored given the same staff and officers (cited in Clough, 1988).

The actions of staff included: neglecting to wash or bath residents and charging them for bathing, probably as a means of reducing the number of people to be bathed; punishing those who complained by leaving one person's feet in excessively hot water for a long time; opening windows and removing blankets at night so that in consequence some residents caught pneumonia and died; some residents were involved in falls following altercations with staff; the bar in the home was used by a few staff, and outsiders who were rowdy and sometimes molested staff or residents (Clough, 1988).

Why does abuse occur on such a scale? Whardaugh and Wilding proposed an extension of Martin's reflective analysis of Hospitals in trouble in 1984. Martin analysed the sequence of enquiries into scandals in long-stay hospitals in the late 1960s and 1970s, just as Clough was to do later in relation to residential centres in 1988, as were Holmes and Johnson on private homes in 1988 and the Harmans on the reports of the Registered Homes Tribunal in 1989. It is an astonishingly painful story. Such an analysis might enable us to see if it is possible to construct a general theory of the reasons for corruption in institutional care. Clough put forward a number of explanations in 1988 of what was to be learnt from the scandals that he reviewed:

> There was a failure within the managing agency to agree about purpose and tasks.
> There was a failure to manage life in the centre in an appropriate way.
> There was a shortage of resources and staff.
> There was confusion and lack of knowledge and frequent absence of guidelines.
> There was the attitude and behaviour of staff, inadequate staffing levels and training and low staff morale.
> Low status was ascribed to the work.
> There was a failure to perceive a pattern in events, individual events being treated in isolation. (Clough, 1988).

Commenting on Clough's findings, Phillipson and Biggs have suggested that they imply a model in which abuse and neglect may be related to three key factors: (a) the home environment; (b) the staff and (c) the residents. In this, they follow Pillemer, who broached this as a provisional model on the basis of his own research (Pillemer, 1988:230).

Phillipson and Biggs went on to suggest that under these separate headings might be included the following factors:

1. *the home environment* - the extent of custodial orientation

(that is, the areas where residents can exercise control over their situation);

2. *the staff* - low staff-patient ratios and staff turnover rate, which themselves may lead to maltreatment if they reach certain levels. They suggest also that the extent to which homes in the statutory sector are integrated into (rather than isolated from) the social services department may be important both in preventing and identifying abuse, a point that is reinforced by Dick Clough in Chapter 12. Staff attitudes, they consider, will be conditioned by wider social attitudes to older people.
3. *the residents*- they highlight two aspects: healthier patients receive more humane treatment from staff; socially isolated residents and patients are at the greatest risk of abuse (Phillipson and Biggs, 1992, 115-16; 1995: 192; see also Bennett and Kingston, 1993: 117-25; and Pillemer, 1988: 233).

Given the importance of Clough's findings, similar as they are to Pillemer's, it is a matter for speculation as to why his report was not published. Indeed a study of the literature surveys (Sinclair, 1988) which were commissioned by Wagner reveals that the findings of the public enquiry reports appear to have been studiously avoided. Eight years previously, Sir Douglas Black published his report on *Inequalities in Health.* which was submitted to the Secretary of State in April 1980. Instead of being published by the DHSS or H M Stationary Office, 260 duplicated copies of the typescript were made publicly available in August Bank Holiday week! Did something similar happen to the Clough report in 1988? The establishment is never keen to make available unpalatable information. Only the tenacity of Peter Townsend and Penguin Books enabled us to read the Black Report at all (Townsend and Davidson, 1982).

Bennett and Kingston have reminded us (1993) that abuse in residential settings can be traced back to practices under the 19th century poor laws. In fact institutional malpractice was not taken seriously until Townsend's *The Last Refuge* in 1962 and Robb's *Sans Everything : A Case to Answer* in 1967. Bennett and Kingston have listed the varied spectrum of abusive and neglectful behaviours encountered in elderly care which have been the subject of American and European studies: invasion of privacy, poor physical care and quality of life, erosion of individuality, resistance to change in geriatric care, inadequate physical working conditions, burnout, organisational factors leading to abusive actions, fraud and the taking of life. They also comment on Pillemer's suggestion that there may be two external factors which influence prevalence of abuse, namely the supply and demand of hospital beds and the unemployment rate which may need to be taken into account (Pillemer,(1988: 234; Bennett and Kingston, 1993: 118).

The Wagner Report on residential care (1988) said that living in a residential establishment should be a positive experience ensuring a better quality of life than the resident could enjoy in any other setting and that the contribution of staff should be recognised and enhanced. So the 1994 report on Standards of nursing in nursing homes by the UK Central Council for Nursing, Midwifery and Health Visiting (UKCC) is welcome. But it revealed that reported cases of misconduct in the nursing home sector had risen from eight per cent to twenty-six per cent since 1990. The report said:

> Whilst the complaints reveal serious professional misconduct such as physical and verbal abuse, they also identify wholly inadequate systems of drug administration, ineffective management systems, lack of systematic care planning or effective record keeping and almost non-existent induction or in-service training (UKCC, 1994:7).

This is a trenchant comment from a professional organisation. How much more difficult is it therefore in the case of professionally unqualified staff and care staff in the independent sector?

Wllcocks, Peace and Kellaher in their 1986 study of 100 public sector homes concluded that the reality of the care home was that the needs of the institution had to be met. The physical environment was not designed to take into account residents' life styles and this was 'a substantial indictment of residential care' (Willcocks et al. 1986: 151), a view that was reinforced by Counsel and Care's report on privacy in 1991.

So what emerges from this review of this starving area of research?

1. It is scandalous that the Establishment, after all these years and countless reports has never understood that it has a responsibility to fund research in this area? The research agenda is wide open in Britain and urgently requires funding.
2. It is clear that management procedures and guidelines are essential.
3. The American studies say again and again that length of

service and the effectiveness of training have a clear relation to stress and burnout.

4. It is clear that we have insufficient understanding of staff-patient conflict. Staff shortages are an important factor in the equation and staff screening and development both need very close attention.
5. We need a theoretical understanding of why abuse, mistreatment and maltreatment occur in residential institutions.
6. Sexual abuse in residential settings is too often a taboo subject. It certainly exists and it merits serious study: abuse between residents, between staff and residents and between residents/patients and relatives.
7. Gender implications also need to be studied more carefully. The majority of residents are women. The implications of gender in elder abuse have been side-stepped for too long. What do we know about women growing old in a male-dominated society? What do we know about women growing old in residential care? What do we know about older women in private care homes, who are managing fees on a fixed income? Losing personal control over admission to a care home is one form of loss, but a residential lifestyle may also depersonalise individuals and all these matters are very relevant to an understanding of abuse(Kenny, 1990: 571-5; Peace, 1993: 140; Lee-Treweek, 1993).

May Sarton, in her novel has her character Caro say: 'I have believed since I came here that I was here to prepare for death ... The best I could hope for was to stand still in the same place' (Sarton, 1993: 125); shortly after that reflection Caro set fire to the home and destroyed it. Of course we can argue that that is far too simple a resolution of Sarton' s plot, but for her, Caro's action seems to be a symbol of the frustration and inner rage that she experienced and it is the feelings of patients, as well as of staff, that we need to understand.

Acknowledgements

I am indebted to Roger Clough of Lancaster University, to Gillian Crosby of the Centre for Policy on Ageing, to Peter Decalmer of the North Manchester NHS Trust, to my colleagues Simon Biggs, Paul Kingston and Chris Phillipson at the Centre for Social Gerontology, Keele University and to Karl Pillemer of Cornell University for their assistance in helping me to obtain some of the very elusive material which I needed for the preparation of this paper.

Five

The abuse of care: The relationship between the person and the place

Mike Nolan

INTRODUCTION

As has recently been noted the world is currently facing the challenges posed by the 'first fully aged societies in human existence' at a time when policy developments and service initiatives are underpinned by a new vocabulary of individual autonomy (Johnson 1995). The response of virtually all developed countries to their changing demographic profiles has been to institute a policy of community care in an effort to achieve more cost-effective use of scarce resource (Dooghe 1992, Walker et al 1993). In achieving this aim increasing emphasis has been placed on the role of the family (informal) system as the mainstay of care provision, often with inadequate support from more formal agencies (Alber 1993). Allied with these developments there has been a reduction in all forms of alternative residential/ institutional provision, especially that provided by the state. Goodwin (1992) suggests that in the UK the National Health Service (NHS) has relinquished any serious pretence to provide a meaningful supply of continuing care. Yet paradoxically these changes are occurring at a time when the proportion of very old people (those aged 85 or over) constitute the most rapidly increasing section of the older population (Dooghe 1992) and these are the group most likely to be in need of some form of institutional alternative. So for example, whilst the overall proportion of older people living in residential or nursing home care is about 6%, this rises dramatically to about 30% at the age of 90 (Victor 1992). Given these statistics the need to maintain a range of care alternatives including some form of institutional care is inescapable (Victor 1992, Higham 1994). However, with the current emphasis on maintaining older people in their own homes the risk is that admission to care will increasingly be seen as a failure and is likely to become further denigrated as a consequence. Indeed the promulgation of community care has served to reinforce an already largely negative image of residential and nursing homes which are increasingly viewed as being universally 'dysfunctional' (Higham 1994).

Such an image is exacerbated by the growing concern about the standards of care provided within such environments and the level of abuse that might exist. Fry (1992) believes that reported abuse represents only the tip of the iceberg and a number of statutory and voluntary bodies have recently added their voices to the growing disquiet (RCN 1992, UKCC 1994, Council for Care 1994). The United Kingdom Central Council for Nursing Midwifery and Health Visiting, the statutory and regulatory body for these professions has suggested that there has been a 300% increase in disciplinary cases concerned with abuse in residential and nursing homes in the last 3 years and that these now represent a quarter of all hearings (UKCC 1994). Against this background there is an urgent need to engage in informed debate about the standards of care provided for the frailest members of society.

Unfortunately, such debate is hampered by the lack of consensus as to what constitutes abuse and the different forms in which abuse might be manifest. For example Lee-Treweek (1994) argues that whilst physical abuse is widely recognised as unacceptable there is little or no concept of mental or emotional cruelty such as intimidation, ridicule or simply ignoring people. It is the purpose of this paper to explore some of the issues and challenges that lie ahead and to seek common ground on which progress can be built. Inevitably such an exercise will raise more questions than it answers and any conclusions reached will be tentative at best. Nevertheless key concepts will be identified and it will be suggested that these must be developed further if meaningful debate is to occur.

CARING FOR FRAIL OLDER PEOPLE: WHAT ARE THE AIMS OF CARE?

The central argument underpinning this paper relates to the

singular failure adequately to conceptualise what the care needs of very frail older people are. Without a basic framework within which to consider key concepts, the quality of life of such individuals cannot be enhanced nor is it possible for an adequate discourse to begin about creating a meaningful and satisfying work environment for the individuals providing care. The unclear or taken for granted manner in which the parameters of good care have been defined effectively inhibits achieving acceptable standards. It is axiomatic that if we cannot define what constitutes 'good care' then its opposite 'abusive care' is similarly vague and nebulous. For example, whilst benchmarks such as privacy, dignity, independence, choice, rights and fulfilment (DoH/SSI 1989) are presented as the hallmarks of good care, what such ideas really mean and how they can be achieved in the context of very high levels of physical and mental frailty is far from clear. As Kellaher and Peace (1990) suggest simply using ideas with increasing frequency does not ensure greater clarity of meaning and Gilloran et al (1993) argue that it is simplistic and misleading to use 'buzzwords' such as autonomy and individuality without agreement as to their definition. In considering the idea of the quality of care provided for dependent older people they note:

> ..... measuring the concept of quality is like a dog's favourite slipper, well chewed, continuously worried, yet remaining undefeated (Gilloran et al 1993).

It is the primary intention of this paper to 'chew over' some alternative views as to what might constitute good and abusive care and to present these as a framework for further debate. In order to provide a common language to describe institutional/residential care the term 'care home' will be adopted (Reed and Payton 1995) to mean both residential and nursing homes, reflecting the increasingly false distinction between such forms of provision (RCN 1992).

CARE HOMES: WHAT MIGHT THE FUTURE HOLD?

In order to set the debate into a meaningful context some key assumptions will be made. Whilst conclusive evidence to substantiate these assumptions is not available they nevertheless have a logic and are consistent with both the present demographic changes and policy imperatives. Therefore, for the purpose of the present argument these assumptions will be presented as axioms, as follows:

- That if community care policies are successful in maintaining older people at home for longer, then those individuals requiring admission to a care home will become increasingly frail;
- Because of greater frailty, lengths of stay will be shorter and older people admitted to care homes will be increasingly likely to die there in a short time rather than living for several years;
- Such factors will fundamentally change the nature of the population in care homes, which will increasingly resemble that formerly associated with NHS Continuing Care environments.

Whilst these changes are unlikely to be entirely universal they nevertheless represent the most plausible scenario in the majority of cases. Accepting this as more or less given also has a number of other logical consequences unless action is taken to counter present trends. Indeed there is already growing evidence that the following changes are occurring:

- There is an increasing mix of cognitively and physically frail older people in care homes;
- Admission to care is occurring largely at a time of crisis, with little or no choice of which home to enter;
- The largely negative public perceptions of care homes is being increasingly reinforced so that entry to care is indeed seen as the 'sign of final failure' (Victor 1992).

Although not the prime focus of this paper it is easy to see how in the above circumstances the potential exists for abuse to begin even prior to entry to care. This is certainly the case in relation to the notion of choice, which is widely recognised as a key determinant of future adjustment (Challis and Bartlett 1988, Biggs 1993).

The ability to exercise choice, to maintain an element of control and to see entry to care as being either voluntary and desirable or legitimate, have been known for some time to be critical variables in the process of relocation (Schulz and Brenner 1977, Rosswurm 1983, Chenitz 1983, Willcocks et al 1987, Porter and Clinton 1992, Johnson et al 1994).

However it is now well established that most admissions to care are made at a time of crisis (Chenitz 1983, Willcocks et al 1987, Challis and Bartlett 1988, Neill 1989, Sinclair 1990, Allen et al 1992, Bland et al 1992, Reinhardy 1993, Hunter et al 1993, Gair and Hartery 1994, Dellasega and Mastrian 1995) often following an acute illness and period of hospitalisation. Due to the sudden nature of the admission, older people themselves are often not involved in the decision-making process and are frequently not even consulted (Neill 1989, Sinclair 1990, Reinhardy 1993, Booth 1993) with the decision either being instigated or made by others, typically family members or professionals, usually doctors (Chenitz 1983, Willcocks et al 1987, Challis and Bartlett 1988, Sinclair 1990, Bland et al 1992, Allen et al 1992, Porter and Clinton 1992, Gair and Hartery 1994, Johnson et al 1994, Dellasega and Mastrian 1995). Furthermore, despite the putative introduction of consumer choice, older people may enter care without alternatives having been discussed (Roberts et al 1991, Sinclair 1990, Allen et al 1992, Bland et al 1992, Hunter et al 1993).

In such circumstances we should begin to question whether the very process of admission itself does not constitute an abuse of one of the key principles underpinning the recent consumer ethos to service delivery, that of choice. It is at this point that a meaningful debate should logically begin. However, this paper is primarily concerned with older people already in a care environment and it is to this area that attention is now turned.

ABUSE OF CARE: WHAT CAN THE LITERATURE TELL US?

It was argued earlier that the future population of care homes will perhaps most closely resemble those individuals who used to occupy NHS continuing care beds for older people, a population characterised by high levels of physical and/or mental frailty. If we are better to understand how the care needs of such individuals can be met then attention to the extensive nursing literature on the topic is instructive from a number of standpoints.

In their introduction to the first major piece of gerontological nursing research, Norton and her colleagues (1962) wrote 'Geriatric nursing has long been recognised as being largely routine work of a particularly heavy nature' and they suggested that the result of this was an emphasis on a task-based work system designed to 'get the work done'. Despite the acceptance of the philosophy of individualised care, the intervening 30 years appear to have done little to improve this situation. A number of studies and reviews of the literature substantiate this conclusion

(Baker 1978, Wells 1980, Evers 1981, Willcocks et al 1983, Janforum 1985, Bond and Bond 1987). This situation was summarised by Kitson (1986) in the following way: 'Without exception, studies have reported how... nursing care was depersonalised, routine orientated and lacking in goal direction'.

The situation appears particularly bleak for the most vulnerable groups of patients in long-stay or continuing care environments. Tomlin (1989) cites Horrocks, who synthesised the results of 12 health authority service reports and reluctantly reached the conclusion that they must reflect the general situation of long-term hospital care for elderly people in the 1980s. He describes ward environments in which privacy was threatened or absent, nursing care was batch-provided with little evidence of individual care, quality of life was extremely poor and patients' minds were numbed by routines and lack of stimulation. It has been recognised for some time that activity within continuing care environments tends to be centred on the provision of personal care, and the meeting of minimal universal needs (Wells 1980), with a dominant work ethos based on getting as much as possible done in the first 3 to 4 hours of each shift (Robb 1985).

A more recent study of the rehabilitative styles of nurses reached an identical conclusion (Waters 1994), describing how a routine approach to care was pervasive, with activity being concentrated in the early morning period. In considering the impact of such care on patients, Evers (1981) utilised the concept of 'warehousing', first suggested by Miller and Gwynne (1972), and proposed that most care for elderly patients was based on 'minimal warehousing', which is likely to lead to depression, humiliation and boredom.

The crucial issue, therefore, becomes: how can the quality of such care be optimised? As Gallagher (1986) notes, despite considerable research in this field, there would appear to have been little improvement in the actual quality of care over the last 40 years. The consistent failure to raise the quality of care received by the frailest members of our elderly population raises a number of significant questions, particularly notions as to what the nature of such care should be and whether there is something inherent in the population in question that makes the delivery of adequate care impossible to achieve. If we are to talk meaningfully about the abuse of care we need to give further consideration to the reciprocal relationship between these two concepts.

CARE: OFTEN USED, RARELY DEFINED

Kyle (1995) suggests that caring is probably one of the most widely used but least understood concepts in the human services literature and consequently as Scott (1995) points out we cannot assume a shared meaning. Moreover even when definitions are agreed considerable work remains to be undertaken before good care can be assured (Scott 1995). Therefore despite the fact that caring has been identified as a fundamental human need (Radsman 1994) there is little consensus on its empirical referents. In synthesising 35 definitions of caring from the literature, Morse et al (1990) outline five main perspectives, with caring being seen as either: an affective response, a human trait, a moral imperative, a therapeutic intervention, or an interpersonal interaction. It is perhaps caring as an affective response, a therapeutic intervention or an interpersonal interaction that are most relevant in the present context.

Such notions would seem to be closely aligned with the wishes of older people themselves. It has long been argued that care environments should be homely and approximate as closely as possible to what people experience in their own homes. In a recent study exploring what older people wanted from care services in their own homes, personal attributes of staff (understanding, generosity, patience and respect) together with emotional support (listening, spending time, fostering hope) were identified as the qualities which framed the provision of acceptable personal care (Poole and Rowat 1994). This is consistent with Scott's (1995) contention that good care is 'constructive' care, that which is technically proficient in instrumental (physical) aspects whilst also being humane, sensitive and compassionate. This, she believes, requires a personal involvement by the caregiver who must be the recipient of care as a 'fellow human being'.

Yet it is the failure to accord frail older people the full status of a 'human being' that appears to underlie much of the so called 'abuse' that exists. Kayser-Jones (1981/1990) suggested that 4 major forms of abuse could be identified:

Infantilisation	treating older people as children
Depersonalisation	rendering their identity as of no value or significance
Dehumanisation	seeing older people as having no human value
Victimisation	theft and abuse of personal property.

Similarly Lee-Treweek (1994) argues that although physical abuse is universally condemned, the more subtle and invidious forms are less easily identified or agreed upon - for example intimidation and ridicule.

As will readily be seen many of the above forms of abuse are related to the basic humanity of the older person. The construction of frail and highly dependent individuals are 'less than whole people' leads readily to the warehousing of care already described which eventually reduces its recipients to 'non-people' (Jacelon 1995) thereby creating a perverse self-fulfilling prophecy. Extending this line of reasoning Dimond (1986) argues that the objectification of care is more easy to rationalise if older people are seen to be 'out of it', as this allows for an impersonal attitude to predominate. Working within such a paradigm makes it legitimate for older people to be perceived as 'feeders' rather than individuals who need help with their nutritional needs (Dimond 1986). Based on his ethnographic study of a nursing home in the USA Dimond (1986) vividly and eloquently describes how 'vitals', that is the important aspects of care, related to physical life and were not concerned with individual biography, emotions and the social milieu. Eight years later and across the Atlantic Lee-Treweek (1994) portrays a depressingly similar picture of life in a nursing home in the UK. She suggests that the motivation behind the activity of the unqualified care staff, who give the majority of 'hands on care', is to present the 'lounge standard patient'. This is an individual who is smartly attired and looks neat and tidy whilst on public display in the lounge. Within their work world the presentation of a 'well-ordered body' symbolised a job well done. In order to achieve this it was considered both necessary and legitimate to be ruthless in the delivery of care. Individuals who did not reach the required 'lounge standard' were confined to their own rooms, but in order to ensure that as many individuals as possible were presentable then 'mistreatment and being hard towards patients' became seen as an essential attribute of the good worker (Lee-Treweek 1994).

Whilst this might represent an extreme form it is nevertheless recognisable as a variant of the 'good geriatric care' described by Reed and Bond (1991) which these authors consider is the goal of care for staff working in continuing care wards for older people. As the usual benchmark of cure was not possible in such wards then 'good geriatric care' was substituted and neat, orderly environment and tidy patients became the criteria for acceptable performance. Such goals lead inevitably to a routine system of care designed primarily to get the work done. This also raises the difficult question of how to create and sustain a meaningful and satisfying work environment for staff. Although the focus of the above studies relates to standards of nursing care there is no doubt that similar situations occur in every environment in which people with extreme frailty, whether elderly or not, are cared for. If we are to address this issue in a thorough-going way then a consideration of the role and value of staff is essential.

THE ABUSE OF CARE: THE VALUE OF STAFF

It is neither possible or meaningful to enter into a discussion about poor care within care homes without turning some attention to the role of staff and the part they play in initiating and sustaining abusive situations. Kayser-Jones (1981/1990) argued that work with frail older people is neither highly valued nor highly paid, a point reiterated by a number of other authors (Dimond 1986, Gilloran et al 1993, Lee-Treweek 1994). Gilloran et al (1993) believe that the lack of challenge provided by such work leads to frustration amongst staff, which is exacerbated by the difficulty they experience in finding meaning and worth in what they do (Pursey and Luker 1995).

According to Lee-Treweek (1994) because of the lack of satisfaction obtained from their work, unqualified care staff, tended to view 'getting back at patients' as a legitimate part of the job, as if in some way frail older people are themselves to blame for the fact that there is little job satisfaction. For qualified staff, nurses in particular, related but different difficulties arise. McFarlane (1976) identified some 20 years ago that nursing has never fully valued or developed its caring as opposed to its curing role. This is particularly relevant to the care of frail older people where few explicit aims have been identified (Evers 1981a) and nurses have often been left with the care that no-one else really values but without legitimate authority to determine care, which remains with the medical profession (Evers 1981a, b, 1982). In order to understand this lack of emotional attachment towards frail older people noted amongst both qualified and unqualified staff Pennington and Pierce (1985) have suggested the concept of 'rust out'.

Pennington and Pierce (1985) believe that individuals working in an unchallenging environment are likely to suffer from what they term 'rust out'. They contrast the precursors of this phenomenon with the more commonly described 'burn out' but argue that the end results are essentially similar in that carers become emotionally detached and isolated from their work. Therefore, whilst burn out results from a highly stressful work environment, rust out is a consequence of the opposite in which 'isolation does not develop in order to escape the agony of high stress but to avoid the tedium of lack of stimulation' (Pennington and Pierce 1985).

More recently, Nolan and Grant (1993) have illustrated the utility of 'rust out' when examining the impact of the introduction of a respite care scheme in a number of continuing care hospitals for older people. The introduction of a number of rota beds in which patients spent 2 weeks out of every 8 in hospital served to raise both the status of the units as a whole and the job satisfaction and morale of individual staff members. Therefore the units were now seen to be serving a more useful function for the wider community and for both qualified and unqualified staff the respite beds were described as having brought a variety and purpose to their work which had previously been lacking.

For qualified staff the regular admission of new patients in this way was also seen to have increased their opportunities to practice more advanced nursing skills. This was noted by one nurse in the following way:

> What is geriatric nursing? Beds, backs, baths and bowels, beds, backs, baths and bowels. No real change and no real challenge. Well, all that's changed recently and I think it's the best thing that's ever happened. (Nolan and Grant, 1993:)

On the basis of their work Nolan and Grant (1993) argue that 'rust out' has empirical validity and should be used as a key concept to help understand and improve the job satisfaction and morale of staff working with the most dependent older members of our society. They also outline a second concept building on the work of Marck (1990) on 'therapeutic reciprocity'. Marck (1990) contends that within any care-giving context a genuinely therapeutic relationship can only develop when there is mutual exchange of feelings, thoughts and experiences that allow for the construction of some form of shared meaning. Therefore at the most fundamental level there must be some form of dyadic exchange if relationships are to develop. The requirements for achieving therapeutic reciprocity (TR) as identified by Marck (1990) were summarised in the following way by Nolan and

Grant (1993) who also identified some of the questions the concept raises in continuing care environments:

- TR is possible in any situation where two people can interact to share either thoughts, feelings or behaviour. Where such exchange is not possible family members may act as a proxy in the short term, but TR becomes very difficult when it is not possible to create meaning in interactions over a sustained period.
- The meaning of any exchange must be sufficient to outweigh inhibiting factors (termed interference) such as lack of privacy, lack of time, or differences in language and culture, etc.
- Caregivers must be sufficiently skilled in facilitating TR and sufficiently motivated to overcome potential barriers.
- Caregivers must recognise that each situation is unique and accept that there are multiple possible meanings. They must therefore be willing to explore and share such meanings with an open mind.

The difficulties of establishing TR with very frail individuals who may have limited abilities to meet the above antecedents are quite apparent. Indeed, Marck (1990) herself contends that particular problems arise when the prospects of progress and interaction are limited and in such situations she suggests that there is a tendency for a custodial relationship to develop. This is a contention which most of the empirical research within long stay/continuing-care patients over the last 30 years would bear out.

It seems reasonable to suggest therefore that if 'rust out' is to be avoided and the prospects for more therapeutic relationships, and subsequently better care, are to be improved, then the goals and purpose of work with frail older people must be made more explicit and such work must be accorded value and worth. Yet given the already largely negative image of care homes and the possibility that such images may well be further tarnished, we need to consider as a matter of urgency, what action should and must be taken to counteract a potentially ever-downward spiral?

THE ABUSE OF CARE: STRATEGIES FOR A BETTER FUTURE

At the most fundamental and most important level there is a need for a balanced yet rigorous public debate on the role and value of care homes and the positive contribution they can make.

Johnson (1995) believes that the economic imperatives driving community care have resulted in a willingness to introduce largely untested and unevaluated policies (including community care itself) and to accept them as well proven remedies. It has been pointed out that it was not until the 1980s that we were helped to 'discover' that living at home was good for us (Lawrence et al 1987) and it was this revelation that resulted in even more negative images of alternative forms of care. Yet as Willcocks (1986) contends, the case against institutional care is incomplete and is based more on historical failure than a realistic assessment of current potential. Moreover, not all older people are universally opposed to the idea of entering a nursing or residential home, particularly as they become frailer (Allen et al 1992, Victor 1992, Johnson et al 1994).

In a lucid and well argued paper Baldwin et al (1993) detail the sustained attack against what they term 'institutional care' but contend that such critiques have been both unidimensional and unidirectional and are guilty of presenting a static view which projects residents 'devoid of their pasts and denied their futures' (Baldwin et al 1993 p70). Developing their arguments further they illustrate that there has been a dearth of comparative studies with similarly frail populations in community settings and an uncritical acceptance of the supposed superiority of community care. They pose the question - what quality of life do frail older people really achieve at home? and they note:

> Many older people at home cope without the benefit of regular care. In such circumstances depersonalisation, loneliness, withdrawal and depression may be common and might in other contexts be described as institutionalisation (Baldwin et al p75).

They suggest that there is a need to adopt a wider and more refined view that takes into account the interaction between dependence, independence and interdependence in the care of frail older people in all care settings.

In a recent, and possibly the first paper, to attempt to quantify how very frail older people spend their time at home Lawton et al (1995) studied a group of highly impaired older people living with a family carer and discovered that they were passive for 81% of their waking day and that only 7% of their time was spent on what they termed 'potentially enriching activity'. Based on these results they question whether in fact such individuals might not have been better off in institutional care. They argue that the challenge for the future is to identify how to provide meaningful stimulation for highly dependent older people in all care settings whether in the community or an institution. This will require a more detailed consideration of the factors contributing to an acceptable quality of life amongst very frail older people and how staff within care homes can simultaneously provide good care whilst achieving an acceptable level of job satisfaction.

Concepts such as privacy, dignity, choice and so on still have an important role to play and have been reaffirmed in recent studies which confirm their importance in other cultures and contexts (Lowenstein and Brick 1995). The challenge therefore becomes how do we achieve these laudable aims at the more extreme ends of frailty where most personal care is carried out by another individual and personal space is frequently invaded. It seems clear from most of the recent literature that the key to quality hinges largely on the nature of interpersonal relationships and the recognition that the older person, no matter how frail, has the status of a human being. It is therefore essential that older people are seen to have the potential for continued growth and development, something which is still conspicuous by its absence in many care settings (Koch et al 1995). Kadner (1994) suggests that intimacy is the essence of a therapeutic interaction and that to achieve this requires the self disclosure of personal information. Therefore as Scott (1995) highlights, constructive care requires that staff perceive themselves as an instrument of care and that they have a personal investment in the people they are caring for. In other words caring has no meaning unless the recipient of care in some way "matters". Scott (1995) recognises that this is a profoundly demanding role in terms of energy, imagination, time and emotion but as Kayser-Jones (1981/90) notes 'A personal relationship between staff and the elderly in long-term care institutions is desirable and essential' (p49). Developing and nurturing such relationships is not however simply a matter of intuition and being a 'good' person, for as Goodwin (1992) points out 'TLC (tender, loving, care) and enthusiasm without proper knowledge and skills is, at best, ineffective and, at worst, disastrous' (Goodwin 1992 p39).

Achieving the goal of therapeutic relationships requires that staff themselves: value older people; have the necessary skills to initiate and sustain relationships and have the appropriate environmental support. An investment in the education of all grades of staff is an essential prerequisite (Carr and Kazanowski 1994), in order to stimulate the intent to care and create the necessary conditions for relationships to flourish (Radsman 1994).

On the other hand it must be recognised that this level of personal investment by staff is emotionally challenging, particularly in situations where older people are increasingly likely to die in care homes (Sumaya-Smith 1995). In situations where staff have acted as surrogate families then death can produce a profound grief reaction especially amongst unqualified staff who need the support systems to deal with emotional responses (Sumaya-Smith 1995). The provision of adequate support for staff is an essential component of a good work environment, if staff are not to exhaust their own resources (Kuremyr et al 1994).

Although the importance of good relationships between staff and older people is well recognised more recently there has been a suggestion that considerably more effort should be expended by staff in actively facilitating relationships between older people themselves. (Reed and Macmillan 1995, Payton and Reed 1995, Reed and Payton 1995). This has been summarised in the following way:

> If our ideas about what it means to be a competent person are partly related to our ability to function socially, then by ignoring the social functioning of older people, we are implying that they are not fully people (Reed and MacMillan 1995).

Once again we are returned to the idea of 'personhood' which Jacelon (1995) citing Bahr (1992) sees as the primary goal of good gerontological care. The complex interaction of factors resulting in good (as opposed to abusive) care in care homes is by now becoming increasingly apparent but there is a need to consider further the importance of providing a purposeful life for older people.

CREATING A STIMULATING AND CARING ENVIRONMENT IN CARE HOMES

As argued earlier by Lawton et al (1995) we need to engage in a far more critical debate about the value of purposeful activity and the extent to which care at home or care in a home provides the best environment. Perhaps more importantly we must move beyond seeing activity simply as a form of diversion and view it rather as a therapeutic intervention in its own right (Lawton et al 1995). This does not mean the blanket application of bingo and group sessions, although these have their place, but the tailoring of activity to individual preferences and interests. Indeed it has been suggested that activity should be viewed as 'the antecedent' of positive affect, the neglected other half of mental health (Lawton et al 1995 p169).

Turner (1993, 1994) has presented a series of arguments outlining the benefits of purposeful activity but if these are to be achieved then such a role must be seen as being both valuable and legitimate. Yet it remains the case that most disciplines eschew activity as not being sufficiently professional and that the only thing uniting varying professional groups is the belief that the provision of activity is somebody else's role (Shaw et al 1988).

Shedding this perception will be one of the major challenges for those working in care homes. It is now untenable that older people in care environments spend the majority of their waking day inactive, yet this remains the case (Nolan et al 1995). It has been suggested that a failure to provide a range of purposeful activity can be construed as abuse (Crump 1991) and this is a line of reasoning that merits serious attention. Unfortunately there is still evidence that staff focus their attention on the more socially able individuals and ignore the withdrawn, or those who are less able to reciprocate (Nolan et al 1995).

What is equally, if not more important, is to value the apparently mundane activities and tasks that will increasingly influence the quality of care that frail older people receive. Several years ago it was suggested that professions were in danger of 'throwing out the baby with the bath water' (Nolan 1987) and that in their desire to establish their professional status the apparently less prestigious roles were increasingly reviled. Yet as Dimond (1986) so eloquently describes the value of such seemingly mundane tasks is often incalculable:

> To learn the extremely slow pace of an old person's eating, or how to vary portions and tastes, these are refined skills, but unnamed, indeed suppressed, by the dictates of the organisation. (Dimond 1986).

To devolve such activities to the least well qualified members of staff, whilst apparently more cost effective, may in fact serve further to disadvantage an already disadvantaged section of the population.

Therefore if we are to monitor standards and to see that they steadily improve, it may well behove us to focus on the mundane rather than continue to use the language of abuse. It has already been suggested, in relation to elder abuse in community settings (Bennet 1990) that abuse is too pejorative a word and is likely to result in under reporting. The concept of inadequate care has been suggested instead. A similar logic might usefully be applied to care homes. Kayser-Jones (1981/90) believes that because standards in care homes have steadily fallen, we no longer know what constitutes good care and 'have come to accept a low standard of care as the norm' (p170). In order to overcome this she advocates a move away from the rhetoric of abuse towards a reaffirmation of minimum acceptable standards:

> Fortunately, scandals, while shocking and deplorable are not terribly common. It is however, the level of care below that which is scandalous that is a great concern to me. It is the day-to-day negligence, the indignities, the dehumanisation, and the unkindness - sometimes difficult to document, and often impossible for regulations to prevent - that make life grim in so many of our nursing homes. (Kayser-Jones 1981/1990 p169).

THE ABUSE OF CARE: THE TRIVIAL DOES MATTER

It has been the central argument of this chapter that poor care is unlikely to be successfully countered until there is greater clarity as to the meaning and purpose of work with those individuals at the extremes of frailty who are increasingly likely to be the major occupants of care homes. This is not meant to represent some nihilistic viewpoint but rather a realistic appraisal of the likely future if community care policies continue unchecked, and operate without even the fail-safe of a critical appraisal of their actual effectiveness.

In these circumstances it is becoming evermore apparent that the discourse of abuse is largely inadequate and that if the term is to be confined to the 'scandalous' then it will serve little useful purpose. It is suggested here that there is a need to focus instead on the apparently mundane and trivial events that serve to define contexts for more esoteric notions such as dignity and fulfilment. In this context the idea of a hierarchy of needs, is a useful heuristic device as it reinforces the notion that until basic needs have been meet the rest are of little significance. This is most certainly not to argue that good care is defined only by the meeting of basic needs but instead that in cases of extreme frailty, physical care needs and social interactions often become inextricably linked. This was vividly and poignantly described by Dimond (1986) in the following way:

> The lesson that nursing assistants' tasks are performed within the context of social relationships was taught to me best by Mary Gardner, a 14 year veteran of nursing assistant work. It was she who told me, in all seriousness that "some shit don't stink". I asked her to explain a bit more what she meant. As she was teaching me to make a bed she made it all perfectly clear. "It depends on if you like 'em and they like you, and if you know 'em pretty well; it's hard to clean somebody new, or somebody you don't like. If you like 'em, it's like your baby". A bit later she made reference to a man with whom she had to struggle every day. "But now take Floyd, that bastard's shit is foul". Through her explanation it became clear that the work is not a set of menial tasks, but a set of social relations in which the tasks are embedded. (Dimond 1986 p1292).

Accepting this basic premise allows for a clearer view of what constitutes poor care to emerge and moves the debate from the sensational to the routine. It also further highlights the essentially interpersonal nature of good care. However, as Marck (1990) has argued, meaningful relationships require an element of reciprocity in which older people have something of value to offer. This is not to reduce reciprocity simply to the level of tangible and equal exchange but is to recognise that as a minimum requirement staff must see frail individuals as 'in it' rather than 'out of it' (Dimond 1986), and be prepared to explore a subtle and complex interdependence. For if older people in care homes are largely reliant on staff for a good quality of care, then staff must also find meaning in such activity if they are to achieve an acceptable level of job satisfaction. Recently, it has been suggested that techniques are now available to provide stimulating and meaningful interactions with even the most cognitively frail of older people, and that this activity can also raise staff morale and satisfaction (Dixon and Hamill 1994, Miller 1995). Such techniques deserve more active development and widespread application. This necessitates the ability to use imagination (Scott 1995) and to see potential in even the most adverse circumstances:

> Although a nursing home is often a chaotic and angry place, there are within each home and within most patients, pockets of creativity, of insightfulness, of competence. Patients are active participants in the setting in complex, humorous and gracious ways. (Dimond 1986).

If we need a definition of abuse, therefore, we might think of it in general terms as being the failure to value and maintain the personhood of an individual. It stands to logic therefore that if we are to avoid abuse we must know an individual as a person, with a unique biography and history that transcends any current physical or mental state. Such a conceptualisation helps to shift the balance so that attention is not focused on which acts of omission or commission are seen as abusive and moves towards a positive agenda to maintain or reconstruct personhood. If however we need a wider framework within which to construct more complex models, and undoubtedly as professionals and academics we will seek one, then the notion of 'failure to thrive' as applied to older people by Newbern and Krowchuck (1994) has considerable potential.

In developing a concept more usually associated with children, these authors argue that failure to thrive also has relevance for older people. In elaborating their arguments Newbern and Krowchuck (1994) contend that whilst failure to thrive might manifest itself in physical symptoms such as weight loss or depression it is precipitated and sustained by a failure of older people to adapt and find meaning in their lives. This, the authors believe, stems from problems with 'social relatedness' so that older people may become dislocated, be unable to give of themselves, have an inability to find meaning in their lives and are unable to attach to others.

Interventions aimed at alleviating such a 'failure to thrive' self-evidently have to address the causal factors and help older people to relate in a meaningful way. Recently, Forbes (1994) has argued that hope should be instilled in all elderly people. Forbes suggests that the role of the carer should be to develop a 'hope-fostering environment'. She sees a meaningful and empathetic relationship which involves active listening and an affirmation of an individuals worth and dignity, despite functional limitations, as essential components of such an environment. A meaningful relationship therefore becomes the crux of good care with older people in a continuing care environment.

The challenge this presents to staff must not be underestimated as it is meaningless simply to berate staff for failing to interact with older people if no common ground for such interaction exists. Crucially however the importance of such activity has to be explicitly acknowledged and accorded not only a legitimate status, but also a valued one. In 1981 Kayser-Jones described the far superior standards of care she noted in continuing care environments in the UK as compared to the USA. Nine years later, in the preface to a reprinted version of her text, she noted with some sorrow that the gap had narrowed considerably and that rather than standards in the USA moving up to match those in the UK, care in the UK was falling to levels in the USA. Dimond (1986) presents a cogent account of how, when care is turned into a commodity, it does so at the risk of a fundamental change, in which the reality of patients' lives become blurred and caring relations remain implicit and unnamed. He argues forcibly that a 'counter logic' must be developed which accords older people a far more active role, not only in terms of their own lives, but as social actors in shaping future social policy. Similarly, attention has to be given to the value of the work undertaken by those providing care. The answer he suggests is not to look for the perfect 'nursing home' that is to construct utopia and work backwards. Nor he believes can complex ideas, in his case the commodification of care, be deconstructed 'en masse'. Rather they need to be deconstructed 'word by word proceeding from the local reality' of the people who experience them.

There is an old adage 'look after the pennies and the pounds will look after themselves'. The same might be said of abuse. If the term is to be confined only to levels of care obviously and grossly inadequate, then it is of relatively little use, for in the abuse of care the trivial does matter.

Six

Abuse of younger and older people: Similarities and differences

Ann Craft

In this chapter I shall be drawing on experience of adults with learning disabilities, and to a lesser extent, those with physical disabilities, although it is worth noting in passing that there is increasing concern about children with disabilities, whose needs are not always well met within current child protection procedures.

One major similarity between adults with learning or physical disabilities and older people who require residential accommodation is their position in society, so often disadvantaged, devalued and powerless. But there is one significant difference – most people would, albeit perhaps reluctantly, see themselves as one day going to be old, but not one day going to acquire a learning or major physical disability. However, and for whatever reason, this expectation has not yet really worked through into effective safeguards for older people who are no longer independent.

Terminology is important – one researcher, Chris Williams (1993), argues that the very use of the word 'abuse' serves to lessen or 'soften' the severity of what are, in fact, crimes against the person – crimes which if committed against other members of the public are called 'rape', 'indecent assault', 'buggery' and to those we should add 'assault' and 'grievous bodily harm'. I take his point, but will use the term 'abuse' in this paper to include a whole range of abusive behaviour and activities, some of which constitute legal offences and some of which represent degrading and inhumane treatment, but all of which are misuses of personal, physical or professional power.

A similarity in the position of vulnerable younger and older adults is the relative newness of our knowledge and awareness of abuse in a way which goes beyond the anecdotal (Craft 1994). How have we come to 'think the unthinkable' and what do we now know from research studies about the abuse of adults with learning and with physical disabilities?

RESEARCH AND OTHER INFORMATION

More is known and written about the sexual abuse of adults with learning disabilities than about their physical, financial or emotional abuse or about any abuse of individuals with physical disabilities.

Physical abuse

It is also worth noting that we know far more about the physical abuse and neglect of American children with disabilities than we do about the physical abuse or neglect of any nationality of adults with disabilities. Some of this work on children in the States (Diamond and Jaudes 1983), together with the study of Buchanan and Oliver (1977) in this country, suggests that in up to 12 per cent of cases, cerebral palsy and/or learning disabilities in the child was a result of physical abuse.

Rusch and colleagues in a 1986 American study looked at characteristics which might be significant as factors involved in the abuse of 80 institutionalised individuals with learning disabilities (although the title of the paper refers to 'abuse-provoking ' characteristics which hints at victim-blaming).

In comparing the abused with the non-abused group they identified six significant differences which affected the resident-care giver interactions and relationships. These were:

- *Level of social quotient*
  The abused group needed more help with living skills and personal care, involving some tasks seen as unpleasant.
- *Verbal ability*
  There were more non-verbal people in the abused group. It may be that they were seen as not so 'rewarding'.
- *Age*
  The abused group were younger and physically more active.

- *Degree of mobility*
  The abused group were more mobile.
- *Self injurious behaviour*
  There were more people who self injured in the abused group, with staff perceiving the necessity to physically intervene because otherwise they would be blamed.
- *The level of aggression*
  Most significantly, the abused group were more aggressive.

For those last two 'characteristics' it may be relevant to wonder which came first, the abuse or the self-injury and aggression.

In Helen Westcott's 1993 study for the NSPCC of abuse of children and adults with disabilities, undertaken from the perspective of the abuse survivor, 11 women and 6 men were interviewed. Eight were physically disabled, nine had learning difficulties. All had experienced physical, sexual or emotional abuse. For the individuals with learning disabilities most of them had been abused both as children and adults. For those with physical disabilities, apart from one case, all had been abused as children. Physical abuse had taken place at home and in hospitals and included beatings, being hit with wet towels, forcibly injected and sedated, and being restrained and isolated in a manner similar to that of pin-down. One man abused as a young person and as an adult by hospital staff said:

> I was put in a straight jacket. I just cracked up in the sideroom. Trying to get ways to tell people what was happening. Punishment was to scrub floors with scrubbing brush. They kept hitting me with towels, stripped me of my clothes – had to wear pyjamas. (Westcott 1993, p16)

Why do we know less about physical abuse? Why have we, in the field of learning disabilities, seemingly 'skipped' the stage of growing awareness of non-accidental injury that the child protection field went through in the 1960's and 1970's, prior to a general awareness of sexual abuse issues? One can only speculate. One reason could be that children in the community – the Maria Colwells and Jasmine Beckfords are more visible and more newsworthy, sadly after rather than before their deaths, than institutionalised adults with learning disabilities. Although we have had our official enquiries from Ely in 1969 through to Ashworth and to Stallington more recently, national coverage was never to the same degree.

Another factor is suggested in the small amount of literature that does exist – within services, where difficult, aggressive, challenging clients are almost inevitably located, the threshold of verbal and physical violence is relatively high. Sundram, in a 1984 American study suggests that minor physical assaults are so close to the norm that front rank staff develop a code of silence and solidarity. British official hospital enquiries have highlighted climates and systems within which misguided interpretations and attempts at 'therapies' or 'behaviour modification' were able to be practised, so a 'programme' for a woman who self-induced vomiting involved her being forced to clean up the vomit with her tongue. Or at Ashworth, where a black patient was unmercifully teased and taunted about his lack of brains and anatomical pictures of shrivelled brains with racist comments scrawled on them were put into his locker for him to find. Or naked patients were lined up to wait in bath queues as part of ordinary ward routine. Or staff feel so pressured that to give themselves what they see as legitimate breathing space for an uninterrupted lunch break, they hitch and restrain a young woman with challenging behaviour by her bra straps to the toilet cistern. So not unnaturally she struggles, and on the last fatal occasion, she strangles. One of Sundram's conclusions was that direct care staff:

> ... see themselves as victims of a larger system that would be quick to punish them for minor abuses but slow to recognise and improve the adverse working conditions that contribute to abusive behavior... (Sundram 1984, p240)

Sexual abuse

It is only relatively recently that we have been able to arrive at figures relating to the sexual abuse of adults with learning disabilities, thanks to the work of Hilary Brown and her colleagues at the Tizard Centre, University of Kent. They carried out a study across the whole of the South East Thames Regional Health Authority for two 2-year periods, 1989-1990 and 1991-1992. Here, I just want to focus on a few of the results. (For definitions and more detail, see Brown and Turk 1992; Turk and Brown 1993; Brown et al 1995.)

Over those four years, 167 cases were proven or highly suspect. Most involved contact abuse. In the first study period, 73 per cent of victims were women, 27 per cent were men, but this altered significantly in the second study period to 57 per cent women, 43 per cent men. The average age of victims was 31 years (range 18-61), most were between 21 and 30 which is similar for sexual assault statistics in the general population. Besides their learning disabilities, 70 per cent had additional disabilities such as physical or sensory impairments. The degree of learning disability was not significant, people with all levels of disability had been reported as victims of sexual abuse. It is recognised that different factors may be at work for people with profound learning disabilities as opposed to those with moderate and mild learning disabilities who are far more likely to be out and about. In over two-thirds of cases, abuse came to light because the victim reported it. In the second study, there was some indication that professional awareness had increased and more reports came from them.

With regard to alleged perpetrators, 97 per cent were men, a gender issue which has enormous implications for training and for male members of staff in the way they are involved in care and the way they feel about that involvement. The alleged perpetrators knew their victims in 96 per cent of cases. In the second two year period 48 per cent of alleged perpetrators were other people with learning disabilities (all men); 13 per cent were family members; 17 per cent were staff or volunteers; 13 per cent were other known and trusted adults. Many perpetrators offended against more than one victim. Abuse happened most often in the victim's or perpetrator's home or in their day placement.

From the first study period, an extrapolation was made to give a figure of around 830 new cases a year of sexual abuse of adults with learning disabilities in England and Wales. It was always recognised that this represented the tip of an iceberg because of the way the figures were collected. After the second study period the figure of 830 has been increased to 1200 because it was found that three-quarters of the reported cases had occurred in 1992. As this is so statistically unlikely it was felt that two out of every three cases were forgotten within a year by services.

Filters to reporting

Formal and informal structures within organisations may mitigate against reporting of, and response to, sexual abuse in services. From their experience in collecting data, Turk and Brown (1993) show us some of the 'filters' to our knowing about sexual abuse. In practice these filters may more accurately be called blocks, because the layers are not necessarily permeable.

At the broad base *recognition* is at its height when adults with

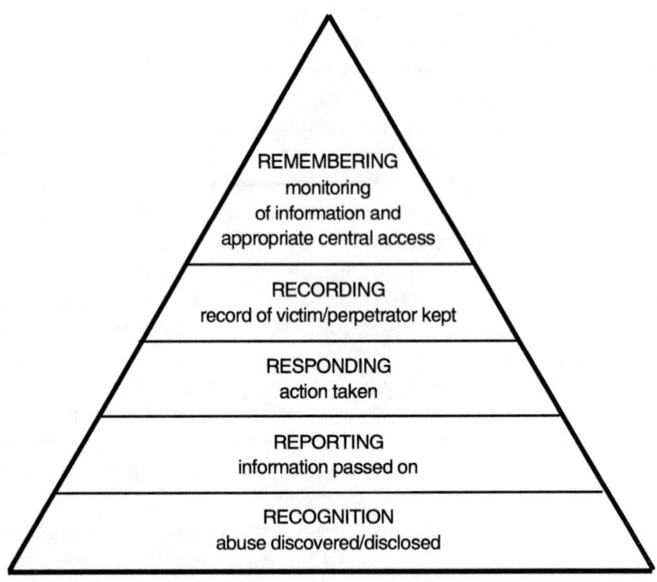

figure 1. Filtering out cases of sexual abuse
(from Turk, V. and Brown, H., 1993)

learning disabilities are able to speak for themselves, so that the recognition is not totally dependent on other people identifying the abuse. When care givers are asked, incidents that are not known to them, or are not believed by them, will not be *reported*. And even if it is recognised, the abuse may go unreported, for example because of the potential reporter's junior position; fear of family break up; fear of causing more harm than good; misplaced loyalty to colleagues; potential scandal for the establishment; fear of job loss. Once abuse has been reported, it is possible that, for similar reasons, no action will be taken or no response made. Whatever their official mission statements, organisations often find it difficult to be on the side of exposure of wrongs because of concern about damage limitation for public reputations. The advent of the market economy may increase defensiveness.

Even if sexual abuse is recognised, reported and responded to, there also needs to be an official recording system. In its absence the service has no ability to utilise knowledge or to plan. Lastly Turk and Brown suggest that mechanisms have to be in place to accurately remember or recall information about sexual abuse cases. Record keeping and remembering are important for individuals who have survived sexual abuse because of movements within services, including staff turnover. Without an official memory, long term safety plans and right of access to treatment and therapy may be lost.

RISK FACTORS

When we think of risk factors there are similarities and differences between our service users. The risk factors outlined below are for sexual abuse and adults with learning disabilities , but they are not necessarily unique to such adults nor to sexual abuse and there are likely to be a number of similarities with the experience of elderly people in residential care.

- *Powerlessness*
  Being devalued, being seen as incompetent children, so that the most junior, newly appointed member of staff has more power than the oldest or most competent resident. We can see this reflected in the way in which assaults are perceived and responded to. For example, Chris Williams (1993) cites a 1991 court case, well-founded enough to have been brought by the Crown Prosecution Service, where the judge said the attack on a 48 year old man with learning disabilities by a member of staff '..was not a serious act of violence' and likened the incident to a parent smacking a child.
- *Pervasive culture of compliance*
  For children and adults with learning disabilities, all too often, doing as you are told is equated with being good. There is a well-recogniseded phenomenon in learning disability literature called 'learned helplessness', but there are also studies showing how elderly people in residential care have decisions taken out of their hands and give up control to staff who can impose informal sanctions and make life unbearable for those perceived as 'difficult'.
- *Small and specialised social networks*
  For so many adults with learning or physical disabilities their social networks are much more restricted than other people's and consist of their own families and/or paid members of staff and other people with disabilities. This can narrow their safety network considerably. George Mabon, gives us parallels in reporting the often low frequency of

visits received by the elderly residents in his Home. (See p117)

- *Contact with specialist services*
  Staff and resident turnover in service networks can and does bring individuals into contact with a large number of other people, in varying degrees of safety.
- *Ignorance of ordinary, 'normal' social and sexual boundaries*
- *Lack of sex education*
  These two do not apply in precisely the same way to elderly people but are significant for many adults with learning disabilities, who may not have an understanding of, or a vocabulary for, sexual parts of the body or for sexual activities. However, this is an area which should not be overlooked in establishments for older people, where staff members' expectations and judgements may lead to situations where consent for sexual activities is being assumed, but not checked out.
- *Perceived lack of credibility*
  Here there may well be similarities between an older person and someone with a learning disability – both can be dismissed as confused, both may have problems with recall, time sequencing and with detail.
- *Limitations in communication skills*
  A significant proportion of adults with learning disabilities have little or no verbal language. While they may communicate distress through depression or loss of skills or through behaviour, this can be misinterpreted so easily. Again, there are similarities with older people who are in varying stages of dementia.
- *Continuing need for partial or complete help with personal and intimate body care*
  A significant number of adults with learning or physical disabilities will require assistance and this will be so for many older people in residential care. While our services have quite rightly gone down the routes of privacy, dignity and respect, most have not, as yet, systematically addressed the risks involved for both the recipients of such care and the carers. [I want to take this point up later.]
- *Presence of additional disabilities*
  Again there are similarities between client groups. Physical or sensory disabilities and increased frailty may make it

difficult to avoid or to escape from abusive situations.

One example which serves to demonstrate a number of the vulnerabilities identified was a Tribunal hearing in 1993 concerning de-registration of a home – *Davies v Powys County Council*. Mrs Davies ran a residential home for eight residents with learning disabilities. Complaints came, not from the powerless residents, but from ex-members of staff. Witnesses described a punishment-oriented regime with physical abuse, neglect, emotional abuse and sexual innuendo. In particular, one resident was provoked into having fits, hosed down with cold water, deprived of medication and left outside for long periods as a punishment. They dealt with his challenging behaviour on one occasion by putting him out of the house in his slippers, in wintry weather, at 7.45 p.m. He was repeatedly refused entry despite his request to come in. He was still there at 9.00 p.m. and when he asked for his drugs, which he normally had at this time, they were refused him. He was still outside at mid-night and told that he was no longer wanted at the home. He set off down the road and was returned by Mrs Davies' son at one o'clock in the morning having promised to behave in future. On another occasion, when he was verbally aggressive, he had his meal removed and put in the waste bin and he was again put outside. He also had records from his much loved record collection deliberately broken by Mr and Mrs Davies as a punishment. When challenged for reasons for some of the forms of punishment described by witnesses, Mrs Davies kept referring to them as 're-directional activities', an innocuous, even therapeutic-sounding phrase which in no way does justice to what was actually entailed.

A SHARED FRAMEWORK FOR RESIDENTIAL CARE

What we in the learning disability field share with services for older people is the overall framework within which residential care sits. Issues therefore arise about:

- The proliferation of services with the growth of independent sector accommodation.
- Purchaser/provider splits and the importance of the content of contracts and the original commissioning.
- The lack of 'teeth' of inspection and registration units.
- The current inability to have police checks of job applicants and the lack of coherence in holding and passing on information about members of staff who are dismissed or

'allowed to resign'. Indeed, we may be passing such individuals backwards and forwards between our respective services.
- The individual and service needs of service users who abuse others. [This is explored in more detail below.]

Those first three points are inextricably intertwined. The market economy may have some advantages over quasi-monopolies and some would say, monolithic, statutory services; and no-one could claim that abuse never occurred in statutory services, but the growth of run-for-profit businesses in the field of care heightens, not lessens, the need for safeguards. The fragmentation of responsibilities between commissioners, purchasers, providers and registration units makes the monitoring of quality and standards a very complex process and there are far too many holes in the fragile net of safety.

While there has been a welcome increase in the last few years in service policies and procedures on adult abuse, in one sense these swim against the tide as statutory services provide less and purchase more. With the split between purchasers and providers it becomes very important for standards concerning policies and procedures relating to suspected or alleged abuse to be written into contracts. Without this there is no clarity about who should do what and who needs to know what. Almost inevitably it is the residents who suffer, and usually in silence. The Department of Health is funding the Association of Directors of Social Services and my own organisation, NAPSAC (National Association for the Protection from Sexual Abuse of Adults and Children with Learning Disabilities), to produce a guidance protocol for Social Services Departments on the Abuse of People with Learning Disabilities in Independent Sector Residential Care.

Within learning disability services the publication *It Could Never Happen Here!* (ARC/NAPSAC 1993) is having a significant impact on awareness of the standards in relation to sexual abuse within residential services which should be accepted between purchasers and providers. It was produced in 1993 by the Association of Residential Care and NAPSAC, with a grant from the Social Services Inspectorate and the Department of Health. It suggests a draft contract and it outlines a clear structure for a model of prevention and response. Although it concerns sexual abuse, much of the model holds good for other kinds of abuse.

The response section proposes four processes:

- Alerting or referring

- Reporting
- Investigating
- Monitoring

The premises are:

- It is the duty of staff at all levels to report suspicions or allegations of [sexual] abuse;
- It is the duty of the service to take reported abuse seriously and to investigate, or have it investigated;
- It is essential for a service to be able to monitor and evaluate the way in which its procedures are working.

In *It Could Never Happen Here!* we followed the suggestion of the Law Commission (1993) and have Social Services Departments as the lead agency, with responsibilities for carrying out investigations of allegations in almost all circumstances, although this might be done jointly with police, inspection units, health trusts, and/or designated officers in larger, independent sector organisations.

Bearing in mind the lessons from child protection about the need to have coherence and co-ordination between the various agencies which may be involved when abuse is suspected or alleged, *It Could Never Happen Here* also proposed the formation of what we called local, inter-agency Adult Protection Committees. It would be a local choice as to whether these committees concerned just adults with learning disabilities or all vulnerable adults, and just sexual abuse or all major kinds of abuse. In Nottinghamshire we are just about to set up such a committee and have opted for a remit of the abuse of adults with learning disabilities. At a later date the parameters of those covered may be widened.

Again, membership of an Adult Protection Committee would be a local decision but should have a broadly based representation. One of the important roles outlined for the Committee is an annual audit and review of the way in which local procedures are working.

PROTECTIVE FEATURES

When a service has officially recognised abuse is a possibility in the lives of residential service users, what are the protective features which can lessen the likelihood of abuse occurring or going undetected? To some extent we are working in the dark, because our knowledge is still new and somewhat fragmentary. We are building up profiles by trying to learn lessons from services or situations where abuse has come to light, but we must always remember that abuse can occur in the best run service, and that unscrupulous individuals, be they family members, staff, volunteers, or members of the public, will target those perceived as vulnerable and perceived as 'safe victims' and will work hard to keep their activities secret.

Managers and staff have a responsibility for the personal safety of individuals within care systems. A chapter in *It Could Never Happen Here* is entitled 'Lowering the Odds'. It sets out some of the features of a service which lessen the likelihood of sexual abuse occurring, or of being concealed. Although the focus of *It Could Never Happen Here* is sexual abuse, a number of the mechanisms hold for other kinds of abuse. Besides the existence of well-understood policies on sexuality and on sexual abuse [and I would argue that the need for such policies holds true within residential services for older persons], I think there are other protective features we can identify:

Service ethos, management style and structure

Explicit and implicit values are generated by service systems. Global mission statements are one thing, but how managers or owners relate to staff, and how staff relate to people in their care, may be quite another. Systems that tend to be inward-looking and self-sufficient are less likely to be open to public scrutiny and bad practice may go unchallenged. For instance, if I were a purchaser for adults with learning or physical disabilities I would think long and hard before placing people in a service which provided both residential and day care, thus employing both sets of staff and lessening the likelihood of outside contact.

Aggressive, or market-based styles of management can make it difficult for concerns to be raised or for complaints to be made and heard, either by residents or by staff. Alison Brammer, a solicitor and lecturer in law at the University of Keele, suggested adopting something similar to the Children Act requirement of an independent visitor programme for elderly people in residential accommodation (1994). Of course, this exists in theory for adults with learning or physical disabilities, under Section 2(5) of the Disabled Persons Act 1986 which permits an authorised representative to visit at any time and to interview in private. However, this section is yet to be brought into force.

Staff recruitment and staff supervision

Those with responsibilities for managing services have to be aware that there are past or potential abusers who purposefully choose to work with those perceived to be vulnerable. This has vital implications for staff recruitment and staff supervision. While we know that most abusers have not been convicted, and therefore would not show up even if police checks were possible on applicants for jobs, careful scrutiny of past work histories and of references sends a signal that here is a service which takes seriously the safety of people in its care. A structured probationary period and good staff supervision can go some way to protecting service users.

Staff training

All staff at all levels will require training related to abuse, giving a clear outline of agency expectations, definitions, signs and signals of abuse and guidance on using of procedures. Some designated staff will need training on supporting individuals who have been abused and on managing the consequences of abuse for everyone concerned.

In Nottinghamshire, joint funding has allowed us to appoint first one, then two Implementation Officers for our Procedures on Protection of Adults with Learning Disabilities. Their rolling programme of staff training is engendering a re-examination of service quality which goes wider than our written definitions of abuse, but which touches upon quite fundamental aspects such as the disrespect shown in a variety of ways to service users.

Self-advocacy and advocacy

A service which facilitates the empowerment of people with learning disabilities is also going some way to foster the protection of those individuals. When people can speak for themselves or for their fellows, or have someone outside the system to speak for them, abuse is less likely to remain hidden and secret.

Sex education

I would not want to claim that offering a positive and comprehensive sex education is a sufficient condition in itself to prevent abuse of people with learning disabilities, but I do think it can play an important part in protection. Sex education gives people a safe forum for learning what is OK and not OK; it teaches a vocabulary for sexual parts of the body and sexual behaviours; it works towards increasing people's sense of their own worth and value.

While sex education per se is not likely to be needed by residents in services for older persons, staff may need training which would cover societal and personal attitudes towards sexual expression by older people and structured procedures for arriving at decisions relating to the consent-exploitation-abuse continuum.

Written procedures on intimate personal care

Most services cater for some individuals who require partial or complete assistance with intimate personal care tasks. Few service managers have taken an honest look at the inherent risks of abuse to people who need that help, or at the risks to the staff of accusations of abuse. Often the implicit assumption is that the 'professionalism' of the person that counts, not the gender. Would a general rule about same sex policy for personal care be a safeguard? Statistics would seem to show that such a rule might protect women, but not men services users as we know that most sexual abusers of both women and men are male.

I do not think there is one hard and fast rule or one solution, but this is an issue services cannot ignore or pretend does not exist.

A recognition that victims / survivors and perpetrators of sexual abuse may exist side by side in the same unit

Within learning disability services, clearly a significant proportion of sexual and physical abuse is carried out by other people (predominantly men) with learning disabilities. How does a service protect those who have already been victimised, or who are vulnerable, from those who use and abuse their fellow residents? How does a service respond to the needs of those abusers with learning disabilities? The situation is complicated because it may well be that they are themselves survivors of abuse, although at this point they are seen as perpetrators.

In the past, sexual abusers with learning disabilities have tended not to be well served. Indeed, in society in general, it is still rare for sexual abusers to receive proper treatment, and we know some of the difficulties associated with this. However, this is a challenge which is becoming increasingly apparent as services get better at naming and recognising abuse.

The Department of Health is funding ARC and NAPSAC to produce a publication on the individual and service needs of people with learning disabilities who sexually abuse others. Not surprisingly, given the undoubted complexities, its working title is *No Easy Answers*.

Inspection and registration

An official protecting mechanism, outside individual services, is of course, Inspection and Registration under the Registered Homes Act 1984 and Residential Care Homes (Amendment) Regulations 1991. But our individual experiences may point to disturbing gaps in what I have called 'the fragile net of safety'. Alison Brammer, in writing about elderly people and the Registered Homes Act, said:

> This [the Act] represents the primary means by which the care of the elderly in registered homes is regulated. A system of quality control and policing is introduced and a framework is provided within which registration authorities can monitor homes, exert powers over them and, in theory, be assured that residents receive adequate care. As identified in a series of Registered Homes Tribunal decisions, the reality is, however, somewhat different..... the laudable intentions and policy of Parliament are undermined by a shortage of resources allocated to registration authorities, insufficient guidance given to those whose task it is to inspect, the restricted nature of legal sanctions available and the tendency of tribunals to favour the interests of the private sector entrepreneur. (Brammer 1994, p. 423)

See also Brown (in press, b) for suggestions of ways in which inspectors and registration officers can use their skills and powers to increase safety for service users.

IS THE JUSTICE SYSTEM PART OF THE PROBLEM OR PART OF THE SOLUTION?

The strong impression within the learning disability field is that the justice system can be placed more towards the problem rather than the solution end of the continuum. I have already referred to some reasons for this. However, there are some indicators of change:

- There is a groundswell of awareness that access to justice is not equal and in all kinds of ways adults with learning disabilities, sensory or physical impairments, and mental health problems are disadvantaged in our adversarial system. A Home Office funded research project on adults with learning disabilities as witnesses is about to report, recommending changes in procedures.

- In response to criticism and disquiet the Crown Prosecution Service is currently undertaking a survey of cases of successful prosecutions relating to victims with learning disabilities so that lessons can be learned.
- A new Parliamentary all-party committee, co-chaired by Edwina Currie and Tessa Jowell, has just been set up to look at the sexual abuse of people with learning disabilities.
- The draft Bill in the latest Law Commission document on Mental Incapacity (1995) would give more powers to Social Work Departments to intervene in relation to 'persons in need of care or protection'. It is to be hoped that this is taken forward.
- A new Whistleblower Protection Bill has just been introduced in Parliament, backed by the Campaign for Freedom of Information and the whistleblowers' support group, Public Concern at Work. The development of written policies on abuse has implications for staff who may 'whistleblow' on colleagues or on the quality of the service. However, the fate of the Bill remains to be seen.
- In many parts of the country, the police are getting much better at taking seriously assaults on people with learning disabilities and more skilled at interviewing people who have special needs in relation to telling of their experiences. (See also Brown in press [a].)
- Lastly, and perhaps we may not be entirely comfortable with this as our society has not tended to be litigious, there are straws in the wind that increasingly, services will be sued for failing to protect people from harm (particularly those known to be vulnerable) or for protecting them in a way which in itself can be harmful. Professor Christina Lyon's work on children with learning disabilities who have severe challenging behaviour has spelled out a number of legal parameters relating to assault and battery, restraint and false imprisonment that adult services cannot ignore (Lyon and Ashcroft 1994).

Be all that as it may, I believe that the clear lesson for services is that although matters may be improving, they should never put all their eggs in the justice system basket. Conviction of a perpetrator or financial compensation for the survivor is only one part of what is usually needed. The actions services take, for example, in terms of long term safety plans, a review of service structure and design and, in the case of sexual abuse, access to therapy for the survivor, can be vital for the person's future safety and physical and mental health.

CONCLUSION

Important similarities between services for older people and for those with learning disabilities, have been the naming of abuse, the beginnings of a body of research in both our fields which means we can speak with increasing confidence, and the formation of organisations such as NAPSAC and Action on Elder Abuse. Such organisations offer support for those working within service structures, they have a lobbying function and channel information and advice into the public debate. We have begun to explore the idea of a coalition of interests.

In summary, uncomfortable and disturbing as it is, abuse is not going to go away. It is a possibility or a reality in the lives of significant numbers of elderly people and those with physical or learning disabilities who are citizens of our country and who use our services. Agency structure and staff procedures need to fully recognise and respond to this fact in order to protect and support individuals at risk. For that we must have co-ordination and coherence within and across services. We must also ensure that we have ways of building on our increasing knowledge and experience. The Lancaster conference has played its part in this.

Part Three:

Structures and Organisations

Seven

What's special about being old?

Evelyn McEwen

For two months this year, I visited my mother every day in hospital. Opposite her was an elderly lady who fascinated me. She obviously had lung and heart problems. She must have been in her 70s and her day was punctuated by the drug trolley and the oxygen mask. As the trolley came round she brought out her list and ordered her cocktail of drugs; as her timer went she put the oxygen mask on her face; and when the paper boy came round she gave him the money for her cigarettes. She was in control of her life, probably exasperating the staff but well up to complaining.

I start there because I have been asked to focus on 'What is special about being old?' An open invitation to a stream of generalisations – I will not entirely refuse it but hope that what I say may trigger some new chord or provoke discussion. It is taken from my experience as Director of Information at Age Concern England, but also from 25 years of living with and listening to older people ... until now I am one myself.

I am 60, but neither 60, nor 70 nor any other age automatically means that there is something special about us.

It may have been the grey beard that caused the young man to say 'You are old Father William'; but often it is when people become pensioners that negative stereotypes start to condition the behaviour of those around them – stereotypes of older people as useless, unhappy, mentally or physically ill, disengaging from life, waiting for death.

How else can we explain attitudes that pervade society, the

State and often professional carers? A study of four pensioner households published by Age Concern England reveals that to live modestly, people would need more then twice the amount of the state basic pension. (Parker 1995). The report was thoroughly researched by specialists such as nutritionists and fuel experts, using thousands of detailed calculations. Would we all not expect to have a radio, a phone and a colour television now? Yet policy-makers who have all of these will nit-pick at its findings. People who probably take at least one foreign holiday a year raise their eyes at a four-day coach trip to Blackpool.

The State pension is kept at poverty level. You talk to pensioners – they think abuse is what the Government does to them. People over 65 are denied benefits such as the mobility component of Disability Living Allowance and access to the Independent Living Fund. Those in residential care who have 'preserved rights' to Income Support would be receiving more money to pay for their care if they became physically disabled before pension age. Yet many young or old will need the same level of care. Some health treatments – for cancer and heart conditions, for example – are less readily available to older people. The whole concept of QUALYS – quality-adjusted life years – is weighted against older people who may have only a few years left to live.

Older people can be quite blunt – what is special about them is that:

> 'there are too bloody many of them;
> they are therefore a 'burden' and a problem'.

These pervasive attitudes can lead to an acceptance of lower standards for older people in institutions. We do not have to go as far back as the sixties, the world described in Peter Townsend's The Last Refuge and Barbara Robb's *Sans Everything*, to find evidence of such attitudes. They are documented in numerous recent publications from Age Concern, NALGO, to Counsel and Care and the UKCC, and of course in stories of abuse in particular homes. Sometimes lack of resources can be a determining factor. Often, the culture within the particular home is identified as the foundation for abuse, but we should not discount the structural nature of this abuse. This affects everyone involved in placing people in institutions, administering their care and providing it, from the Directors of Social Services and the hospital administrators downwards. It leads to collusion which makes neglect an accepted norm.

Abuse does not stop in the hospital or the care home; it is perpetuated by politicians who do not ensure that sufficient resources are made available to fund the services which people need, thus leading to overstretched staff trying to cope in situations where abuse becomes inevitable.

Recently, I know most about that structural abuse from my mother's stay in hospital; an elderly lady was put in a four-bedded ward, where the other patients were elderly men without her permission being sought; people with hearing aids were not helped to put them in; people were put on commodes and left on them. Such abuse is created because hospitals are so short staffed. My mother, who had dementia, fell twice because of this and ended up with a contusion on the back of her head. The nurse in charge of her care was said to have cried at the thought that I might complain, illustrating, perhaps, how we expect staff to work within the structural abuse of the hospital and how they learn to accept it without thought. The ward manager begged me not to complain because it would mean more paperwork and less patient care ... and 'surely I would not want that'.

There is something special about people living in institutions: they are more likely to be physically or mentally frail, dependent, and therefore vulnerable to abuse by others. The 1988 OPCS Survey found that amongst people aged over 85 in institutions, 88 per cent were in severity categories 5-10 and 51 per cent in categories 9 and 10. To illustrate what that means from the survey: severity category 9 is an elderly man with arthritis of the spine, who cannot see or hear well, loses control of his bladder, and cannot get in or out of bed without help. Severity category 10 is an elderly lady who is 'senile', loses track of what she is doing, finds it difficult to understand people, loses control of her bowels once a week, her bladder once a day, cannot get in or out of bed alone (Martin et al 1988).

Today far more elderly people are likely to have such severe disabilities; their dependency will be not only physical but often emotional, so that withholding warmth can itself be cruelty particularly for those who have no family or friends left to care for them.

Being old will mean that our attitudes will have been formed years ago when the world was different; they may even have been formed in different countries – hence the importance of an understanding of ethnic minority elders in care homes.

So, too, it is important to understand the attitudes of the majority of the population. Many staff in care homes were not brought up in Britain, and it is important that we consider their need for training rather than brush it aside because such a consideration is not politically correct. All staff need to understand the social history of our society, how people like to be addressed, where their dignity lies, and even that they do not (if a woman) want to be cared for by a man.

To look for an understanding of old age in the community in which the resident lives and to ensure that they do not meet cruelty is not merely a question of stopping the behaviour of deviant individuals. It is about ensuring that respect for older people is embedded in our culture, as well as in the institution. It is not enough to think that elder abuse is about stamping out extreme physical abuse. What, after all, stops us being cruel and abusive to each other?

I offer two pointers. Firstly, it is our moral values (which I have illustrated with Christian examples). Do we now believe the words 'blessed are the meek'? I often wonder if we ever did. 'Honour thy father and thy mother that their days may be long in the land which the Lord thy God has given.' In a study of staff behaviour in one nursing home it was found that physical abuse was not acceptable but mental and emotional cruelty was: punishment, particularly withholding care, was commonplace. (Lee-Treweek 1994). And what of 'Thou shalt not steal'? Financial abuse is one form of elder abuse which is particularly prevalent. In Nye Bevan Lodge 'pilfering of residents was a regular activity' (Southwark Social Services 1987).

As an individual who has been a carer, I know that it was the moral constraint which brought me up short when I uttered 'cruel words' to my mother. Without this, older people are at risk because they are special in their frailty and dependency in that like children they may not be able to retaliate. Fear is a powerful inhibitor of abuse – and life involves a cycle of fear; as the child grows the parents know the child may become strong and wallop them back, verbally express disgust at a parent's conduct, or report them. When older people become dependent those caring for them may feel less fear: the older person cannot hit back, they may have no visitors to speak for them, or the relatives who could are, like parents with their children at school, afraid to complain for fear of reprisals. In these circumstances, the attitudes of staff to older people become vital, as does an honest recognition by society of the devoted care that is needed.

A small group of older people will themselves be abusers because of the violence shown them throughout their lives, or now because of physical or mental illness. In one study 5 per cent of staff in homes for elderly people and 12 per cent in homes for those who were mentally ill were found to have been severely physically abused by the residents (Eastley et al 1993). We must respect the care workers, particularly care assistants, who work most closely with older people in care homes. They are often denigrated by those who could better spend their time trying to enhance their prestige – and of course we need to pay them a decent rate for the job!

You can see that I do not believe that what is special about old age is a halcyon vision of everyone actively engaged, fit, and so on, until they drop dead (although that is what many of us would wish and will be what happens to many).

What can make old age 'special', if 'special' is taken to mean 'excelling' in some ways, is:

- living life to the full as we wish and not being constrained by societal attitudes;
- coping with disability and ill health and showing that I am still 'me' – why else do we always describe the other person as old?
- seeing life as a cycle in which death is its final fulfilment.

In fact 'growing old gracefully', to use an old-fashioned term.

Those who are around us, from the Secretary of State for Health to the youngest care worker, can help to ensure that we do so. The cry for more resources lets no-one off the hook; it confirms that we are all in this together if older people are to be treated as 'special'.

Eight

The organisational underpinnings of abuse: Implications for abuse of individuals

Elisabeth Henderson

It may be surprising to find a management consultant contributing a chapter on elder abuse. The explanation is that I was called in as a consultant to help an Officer in Charge (OIC) of a residential care home and an external line manager in their investigation into sexual abuse amongst older people in the home. The experience provided me with evidence for the analysis that is developed here.

Why was I involved? Why was this contribution thought to be important? The value of the organisational perspective is that it engages us in a form of thinking that shifted us as a team away from a purely personality focus. This enabled us to ask: What is it about the environment which allows abuse to occur?

It is important in this context to remember how and why we all know the names of residential institutions which have 'gone wrong'. These homes loom large in the history of residential work. Yet, every time a scandal hits the headlines, the focus is primarily on the personal circumstances and the individual psychology of those involved. The scope of our investigation needs to be broader to include a wider range of contributory ingredients. The central question, I will therefore address is as follows: What is dysfunctional about organisations which allows abuse in residential homes? My approach, therefore, is analytical, not only descriptive.

In order to fully concentrate on the organisational perspective, there are a number of fascinating contributory ingredients to the situation which I shall not however examine.

So for example I shall *not* address the psychological drives which impel one old person to treat [mistreat] another in some way – even though it is important to be aware that abusive attitudes and behaviours toward others can, in response to primitive needs, resurface in old age. And the issue of whether continuous abuse over a lifetime may show up in the contained environment of a home is another.

Nor shall I discuss the emotions and reactions of staff – though the realisation of what is happening under their noses must be confusing and disturbing. If not, then the non-reaction by staff would leave one to wonder whether they are able to care for people in a very dependent phase of life.

Nor will I talk about the reactions of relatives and their connection with the person in the residential home. Knowing that their relative is involved, whether as an abuser or as a victim, may trigger anything from anguish due to their love, guilt due to mere duty, to distaste and blame if they wish to distance themselves not only from the abuser but also sometimes from the victim.

This reaction of distancing themselves may be relevant to the theme of this paper. Relatives may have an inkling 'that something is up' but miss the cues, changes of mood, the 'odd' things the resident describes. The relative may find it difficult to distinguish what is serious amongst, what may seem to them to be, the ramblings of an old person. On the other hand, relatives' own feelings about organisations may also be triggered:

> I can't take this up – the authority would never let this happen. If I do take it up I will get punished – the home will retaliate by expelling my relative – dumping him/her back on me and I cannot cope.

Nor will I discuss the role of other professionals outside the home, important though it is to talk about their reactions. How open are those in outside agencies to thinking that 'responsible' authorities can unknowingly house, allow or indeed cover up abuse against residents?

What I *shall* focus on and address in this paper is how an institution can know that abuse is taking place and yet, knowingly, let it go on. My suspicion is that major or minor abuse, or even simply painful experiences for residents, not infrequently occur. It appears that staff, managers, professionals and officials can be caught up with organisational attitudes which prevent them from doing what they feel to be right, even when this causes them to experience moral distress and confusion.

As I have stated already, relatives also may be intimidated by the organisation. It may be more believable to them that an old person's mind is wandering than that the home and the 'officials' are failing in their responsibilities.

What is it about organisations and our attitudes that presents even the best of us with such dilemmas that we distance ourselves from what we feel and know to be right? I would suggest that everyone has had this experience. The telling difference is whether or not we face the moral issue, confronting a natural tendency to locate responsibility elsewhere, or take responsibility, deciding for ourselves how and when to compromise.

CONCEPTS FOR UNDERSTANDING ORGANISATIONAL POWERLESSNESS

Organisational powerlessness is pervasive and belongs to many more types of organisations than simply residential homes. Later I will come to issues that are specific to homes.

We will look at some concepts for understanding how the dynamics of organisations influence day to day activities and decision making. These are:

1. The individual and emotional aspects of the 'group or organisational Self'.
2. Group culture in organisations.
3. The impact of functional/structural arrangements within the organisation.

The individual 'group self': how the deal is struck

We need to review how individuals relate to a group, and therefore to their own organisation with its dynamics.

If we take a moment to think how it feels to join a new group we can be in touch with the emotions groups engender. At a very simple level the individual coming into a new group is alerted to danger as well as a range of other emotions. The individual can feel 'the group is bigger than me; it can expose me, embarrass me, show me up'. This particular experience translates into concerns about belonging to or exclusion from the group. It may be that during our early learning and socialisation through the organisation of family and school, personal deals or accommodations are struck. The deal may be internalised in terms of subordination to the requirements of the organisation in order to survive or belong. Sometimes people rebel against a group simply because they cannot bear the tension of belonging on other people's terms (not only because the terms may seem to them to be distorted).

People can be timid in relation to the organisation. They may feel powerless, giving their sense of value over to the organisation, valuing themselves by how they are valued. Others are able to retain and develop their sense of personal judgement, constantly discriminating what is due to themselves on the one hand and to their allegiance to the organisation on the other. But to do this is difficult stuff.

Too often the deal that people make with the group is an acceptance of hierarchy as meaning fundamental division between superior and subordinate. If the experience of dependency as subordinate has been painful, the individual can carry into new situations:

- frozen (repetitive) personal responses;
- expectations of moral judgements against themselves;
- inflexible moral precepts;
- a set standards of how one should behave in organisations.

Thus, instead of individual negotiation, testing out what is and is not possible, individuals behave how they believe they 'ought' to behave. The concept of 'group self' is created and acted upon. An individual may develop the confusing belief that it is a greater disloyalty to 'tell' on their boss than disloyalty to the residents not to protect them. Thus, they live with a situation that horrifies and causes them even more stress.

Dependency / group culture

In the work of W. R. Bion (1960), a number of dynamic cultures are described. The dependency culture described here is the one most likely to operate amongst staff since it mirrors the nature of work in residential homes for older people.

It is easy to know when the group is in the grip of a dependency dynamic: everyone tends to be clear about the short-comings of leader/manager, and analyses them *ad nauseam*, probably in the pub. Nevertheless they safeguard the leader as if questioning leadership is the same as dismantling all aspects of power, hierarchy, authority and all that will be left afterwards if this is questioned is simply chaos. This dependency dynamic illuminates the paradox of such intense loyalty to a leader whose short comings they are aware of.

A dependency culture is one where individuals in the group have a shared belief that the leader ought to be the ultimate caregiver, leader and allocator. This belief leads to a shared dynamic by the people at the top and bottom: it is experienced as dangerous to face up to the fact that the [any] leader/manager cannot be all the above. In a dependency culture, it is felt that to question the leader's capacity would break down the whole system's capacity to deliver care. So individuals inhibit their concerns or complaints about the leader/managers, however much they may grumble, stifle their own creativity and try and behave in ways that 'respect' the leader, as though they are trying to enable that person to be what he or she 'should be'.

The operational effects of the functional / structural arrangements of an organisation – and the unattended consequences.

In order to illustrate this, I will give an example from my own experience at a boarding school. There to my surprise I learned you needed to have one best friend (or three) but not two. Every few days for over an hour the entire school attended a meeting which required that children walked through the town in twos. This necessitated that each person had one other girl to walk with. Threes overspread too far across the pavement. These arrangements must have seemed very practical to the school authorities. Yet their impact had an effect in that they formed the emotional and social life of the children at the school.

A basic example in one residential home was the issue of laundry. This is such an apparently low level task that day-to-day running was left entirely to domestic staff. Yet a survey in the home found that the single most significant improvement for residents would be in laundry. For residents a highly upsetting factor of institutional life was not getting back your own clothes or having them entirely lost and having complaints seen as fairly frivolous.

Administrative arrangements can have disproportionate effects (from their seeming importance) on the emotional life of the people involved.

The phenomena I am describing is how functional/structural arrangements provide for and fashion personal relationships, organisational beliefs and peoples' feelings and beliefs about how they ought to behave later.

I will relate this to how a local authority's chain of command can impact on the residential homes.

THE IMPENETRABILITY OF THE RESIDENTIAL HOME

How do these three concepts relate to residential homes? Particularly how do they shed light on the way in which abuse or disagreeable, unhappy experiences can be perpetuated by a regime?

Dependency and confusion

We need to look at residential staff and the kind of group self and level of understanding staff may possess of how organisations run. As I have described earlier, by 'group self' I mean the expectations each person has of a group: how the group operates, how people are dealt with, how they themselves will be treated, how they should behave in order to do well and be approved of. Let us now look at the situation which arises if and when care staff or officers in charge have a negative group self or low self esteem coupled with little understanding of the effects of organisational functioning – and how they may then react.

Care staff

Particularly at the day to day level care staff may:

- have little personal confidence;
- relate one-to-one with residents but have little concept of how groups function;
- have little understanding of how organisations run;
- be easily intimidated in the new setting due to old experiences;
- feel that they have no right to put their foot out of step;
- easily experience being evaluated by those above;
- have a very strong sense of the economic power of the boss over them;
- tend to globalise the power of the boss as total within the home.

Officers in charge

There is pressure on the manager to conform to the image of being the boss. It is not often discussed how little experience of organisation many people heading residential homes may have.

For many their only real management training is the process of rising through the organisation to the top. Managers too may simplistically believe the relation between top and bottom is that power is held by the top and, *in extremis*, the bottom (staff) only have rights when given to them by the boss. If you come up through the system with these beliefs and arrive at the top of an organisation this causes a double-edged pressure. On the one hand, there is a terrible requirement on you to behave like a 'proper' boss. Your own internalised belief system demands you show those above and below you that you are this boss and you have the controls. On the other, when you feel unsure of how to proceed you cannot do the natural thing (perhaps ask for help) as this would show you are not 'up to it'.

I should like to make the same point through a more benign illustration of how in a dependency culture, authority is allocated to the top in its entirety. Let us take the example of a warm empowering OIC who encourages contributions, inputs, and participatory team meetings. Frequently two factors occur together: first, the style and the involvement are appreciated and staff feel appreciated in turn; secondly, nevertheless this regime is seen as his or her system; staff still perceive it as how the OIC likes to run the home and not as a joint system in which all the members are collaborating

The danger is that a percentage of OICs and staff not only cannot imagine operating a more open participatory system where staff [even residents] have a voice, but believe such a voice would be dangerous, breaking down the role and status of the boss, and therefore the home, exposing both as inadequate. In such situations the attentions of a Senior Professional Officer (SPO) can be experienced almost as a form of sabotage, to be repelled or stonewalled. The outsider is excluded.

The management system

A residential home is a part of a local authority structure with all its functional/structural arrangements. There is a widespread management fallacy, often pictured in the organisational chart with its spans of control, that the hierarchical arrangements of the local authority reproduce themselves in the same way within residential homes. Line management arrangements are thus thought to be sufficient safeguard for the health of the home and for improving standards. We need however to examine:

- whether hierarchical thinking really does illuminate the

real situation;

- how the benefits inherent in the line of command can mesh with the benefits of co-operative working.

What are the misconceptions of how hierarchy works in residential homes? On paper it looks as follows:

Fig I Formal organisational structure chart

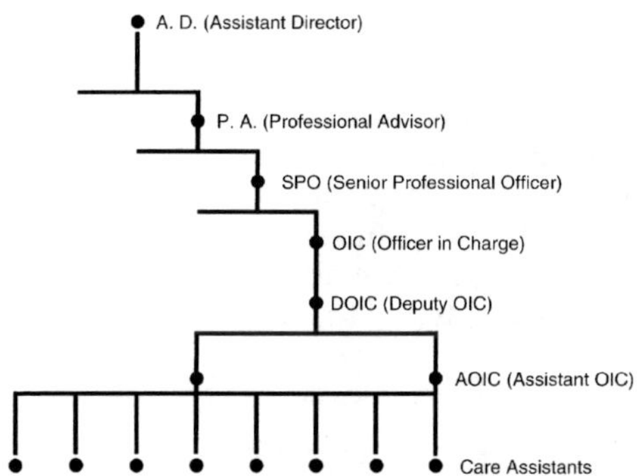

But a residential home is a very different system with its own blocks and filters.

Fig 2 The link between the residential home and the local authority system

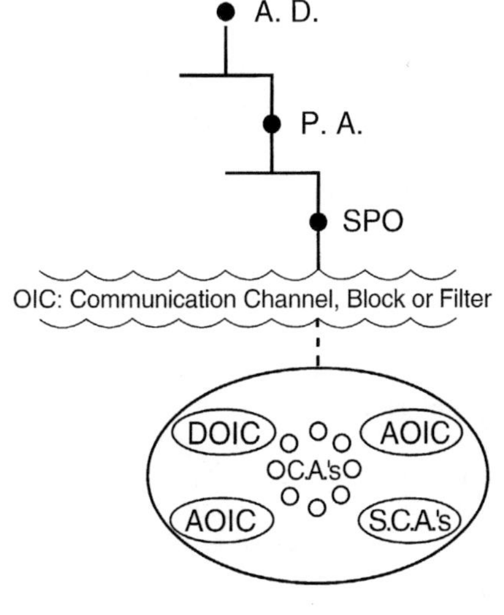

THE TWO HIERARCHIES

The County or Town Hall Hierarchy [Figure One] has a downwards form of instruction and direction with occasional upwards communication. It is a formal bureaucracy.

The Residential Organisation [Figure Two] functions very differently. It is centralised and directed at the top with staff forming a fairly interchangeable pool of workers. The work requires shift work and the model of organisation is not a formal bureaucracy.

Information and access between Town Hall, and Residential Home, relies on the permission of the OIC if hierarchical channels are used. At present this choice of disclosure really depends on the personal style and willingness of the OIC.

In fact because of the type of work, a residential home can function like a matrix with different groups of staff across levels providing teams of care, often all 'mucking in' under the either the 'fiefdom' or 'leadership' of the OIC as the case maybe.

Fig 3. Matrix: shift and teamwork in the home

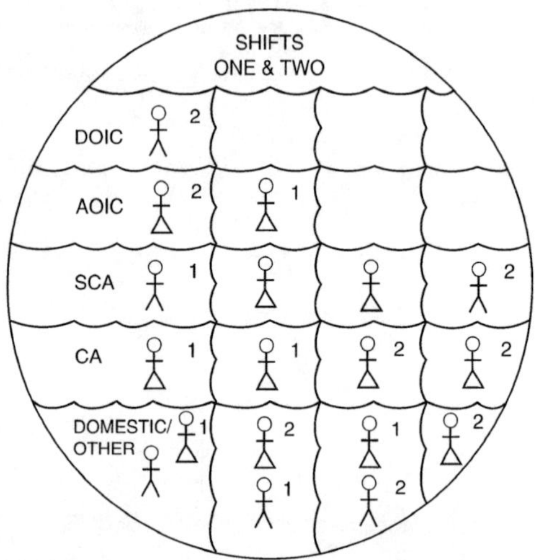

THE OIC AS A BLOCK OR FILTER OF COMMUNICATION

The critical issue is the structural potential for the OIC to interfere with communication. As we have seen, there is an assumption in the local authority that a residential home duplicates its own hierarchical model in its management norms and systems. The filter between the OIC and SPO may be regarded from above as not very different from any other hierarchical interface. It is in fact intrinsically different because the internal, isolated nature of the home ensures that the OIC position is pivotal.

This internal isolation is compounded by two factors. Firstly, part of the ethic of bureaucracy is that higher management 'trust' middle management. Direct access from above to staff below the middle manager is equated with interference or 'distrust' of the middle manager. Therefore, there comes into action a simplistic further equation: such access would be 'obviously' unsupportive, sabotaging the authority, role and status of that manager.

Secondly, in a bureaucracy, hierarchical authority is relayed downwards tier by tier. But, as we have seen, the nature of residential work is such that all staff are interchangeable and are functionally and necessarily work-dependent on the OIC and/or deputy. The OIC role is very powerful both as supervisor and arbiter.

The OIC is therefore in a key position to either block or enable information flow. So the following scenarios exist:

1. Information from SPO can simply be blocked by 'bad' relationships.
2. The OIC can fail to consult with the unit, that is with the staff in the home; so, despite an apparently 'good' relationship between SPO and OIC, information actually does not reach the unit. The unit is not touched by wider contacts and expertise; it becomes 'a little empire'.
3. There is no backward flow of information from the unit to the outside as communication outwards can be totally dependent on the OIC. Thus not only the residents but also staff are effectively operating in what Goffman calls 'a total institution'. Such an institution is defined as a law unto itself, with little access to external reference points or effective intervention from outside.

Disclosure of abuse therefore appears to pivot on the use of the power and position of the individual within the hierarchy.

CONCLUSION

An individual's ability to prevent abuse or to ensure its secrecy depends on his or her position within the hierarchy. Victims, at the lowest point of the hierarchy, are often powerless to prevent the abuse because of their physical and mental condition. The staff group occupy a variety of levels in this hierarchy. This may be due to their own personal power and to the power invested in their position. They too can find themselves in a powerless position in terms of preventing abuse. Some may be frightened of the perpetrator, some may have direct experience of how power can be used to prevent disclosure. Generally, power structures can enable managers who so wish to block information and to prevent it from becoming widely known, particularly outside the establishment.

So, in conclusion, it appears that it is highly possible that an organisation will perpetuate abuse, avoiding its prevention and exposure, if a situation prevails where:

1. the group self of many of the staff is one of subservience and low self esteem;
2. the dependency culture is such that loyalty and subordination to the boss is seen as proper and the alternatives are seen as dangerous;
3. the OIC feels that the only way to continue to hold together her/his identity as the boss, over even a creaking ship, is by ignoring signs of fragmentation; and
4. the chain of command structure in the authority does not recognise how one person controls a pivotal point in the system.

NEXT STEPS

The disciplinary position

In my view and that of the team I worked with, a structural functional analysis of the departmental disciplinary process in the social services department is needed. The process should be designed to avoid scape-goating individuals for involvement when within their system it would have been hard for staff at certain levels to behave otherwise. This process of disciplinary action might focus on those who have the power to act differently, rather than according to the traditional model where only the actions of individuals are highlighted within the disciplinary process. It might be possible to reframe the concept of discipline: 'it is the system itself which needs the disciplining.'

Prevention

How can we address the problem of prevention? Is it possible to train staff not only in care skills but also in a justice model of the home as an organisation – where loyalty is to the task, and the needs of the old person would be paramount?

Will the local authority [in these days of straitened finance] invest in opening up the OIC constriction point in the hierarchy? Because it will cost. Can there be something like active Action Learning Groups for OICs and their deputies across an authority? Could the authority invest in professional officers who both are required to and do have the skills for sensitively co-working in a consultative mode with the OIC inside their Home, together with their staff?

FINALE

In this chapter I have touched on some critical factors in the functioning isolation of the home and therefore in its potential for failure to disclose. Maybe the next critical stage is to identify the development of an open system of governance within the home, without, of course, unintentionally jeopardising the benefits of its sense of identity.

Nine

Do social services departments contribute to the abuse of older people?

Mark Lymbery

INTRODUCTION

Olive Stevenson (p.173) notes that abuse of older people in the residential setting may be manifested in four different ways:

staff	>	resident
resident	>	resident
resident	>	staff
local authority	>	resident

In this chapter I seek to address the implications of the fourth category – the potential for local authority social services departments (SSDs) to contribute to the abuse of older people who either live in the SSD's own residential care homes, or are funded by the SSD in independent sector residential care or nursing homes under the provisions of the National Health Service and Community Care Act 1990. Under this act, SSDs have the *duty* to assess needs and arrange care services (HMSO, 1990); implicit in the Act and all subsequent guidance is that the SSD has the responsibility to look after the welfare of all people for whom it has arranged services.

It may seem paradoxical to suggest that an SSD could contribute to the abuse of those people for whom it accepts this responsibility. However, in this chapter I argue that a combination of a lack of understanding and financial expediency creates a favourable climate for abuse. It is also suggested that the existence of abuse may be denied, for reasons which are predominantly political. Further, the chapter claims that some policies and actions of SSDs may in themselves constitute a form of direct abuse of older people. I do not presume that any SSD engages consciously in direct abuse, or actively seeks to create the circumstances where abuse may flourish, but rather that abuse may be the unintended consequence of a range of policy decisions. Indeed, many of the acts of an SSD which may be considered to be abusive stem from financial pressures over which the SSD has limited control. However, the fact that the SSD may not intend the abuse does not lessen its impact on those older people who have to suffer its consequences. It is therefore important that each SSD recognises the possible impact of its policies and practices on older people, so that the incidence of abuse may be reduced.

A general note on the source of many of the arguments in this chapter is appropriate here. Between 1992 and 1995 I worked on all aspects of the implementation of community care policies. During that time I had many opportunities to discuss policy and practice issues with a range of others: policy-makers, inspectors and practitioners in the local authority, health authority and independent sector. The issues which are described in this chapter stem from such discussions; the interpretation of their consequences as abusive is mine alone.

CREATING THE CLIMATE FOR ABUSE

A number of factors which may contribute to an abusive climate can be observed in SSD direct care provision. Despite the requirement under legislation that SSD residential care be inspected to common standards, the lack of power of registration and inspection units over SSD homes means that the common standards are difficult to enforce. Consider, for example, the issue of staffing levels: inspection officers in several SSDs have noted that staffing levels in SSD residential homes tend to be lower than would be acceptable in an equivalent independent sector establishment, taking the dependency levels of residents into account. Lower staffing levels imply higher workloads and increased stress levels for staff; 'stressed-out' staff are more likely to act in ways which are abusive of the resident group.

In many SSDs the management of residential services

presents a continuing problem. It is difficult for outsiders to penetrate the closed environment of a residential home; considerable autonomy is vested in the officer-in-charge who has the power substantially to control access in and out of the home. If the officer-in-charge's line manager is not experienced in residential work, this process may not be understood – and, if not understood, will not be effectively handled. The problem may be compounded where the line manager neither supports nor values the concept of residential care (see Dick Clough, p.142). With an increasing emphasis on generic management in SSDs, some of the specialist skills required to manage a group of residential homes may be in short supply as more middle managers come from a field social work background.

Staff working within the residential environment may feel that there is little value placed on their task, and that their jobs have only limited security; the numbers of SSD old people's homes which have closed in the past few years bear testament to the validity of such views. The possible consequence of this is clear: staff whose morale is low are more likely to act in ways which are abusive to the resident group, either directly or indirectly (see Glendenning, pp.42-43).

It is commonly believed that the dependency levels of people admitted to residential homes in both the independent and local authority sectors are increasing as SSDs seek to enable more people to remain within their own homes with community-based support, in accordance with a key objective of the legislation (DoH, 1989). However, the increase in dependency is not necessarily mirrored by an increase in the fees paid by SSDs for residential and nursing home care. According to a recent survey, the major determinant of fees for residential and nursing homes has been 'local market conditions': that is, fees are broadly higher in high cost areas and lower in low cost areas, and do not necessarily reflect individual dependency (Community Care Market News, 1995). The financial circumstances of local authorities must be considered as a factor in the fees paid for residential and nursing home care; several authorities, for example, Sheffield, Gloucestershire and the Isle of Wight which have had the most publicised financial problems in recent months, are now paying less than the Department of Social Security (DSS) 'baseline' rate for residential and nursing home care (Community Care Market News, 1995). Given the perceived increase in residents' dependency levels, one could conclude that the fee levels which many authorities pay for residential and nursing home care are no longer sufficient to provide good quality care. (I am aware that this argument rests on a contested point: the adequacy of the DSS levels as an accurate indicator of the costs of care.)

Registration and inspection units do have the power to require independent sector homes to raise staffing levels if the overall dependency of residents increases, but higher staffing levels mean greater overheads for homes; if the income received by homes is not also increased this either will mean a reduced profit margin for the home owner or a trimming of services elsewhere. (In a highly competitive environment, it is unlikely that homes will refuse to admit residents, whether or not they have staffing levels adequate for the needs of particular residents.) A trimming of services may lead to a reduction in the wage levels paid to staff, a reduction in the quality and quantity of food, or a general reduction in care standards. All of these consequences are either directly abusive for residents, or serve to create the climate for abuse. The SSD which establishes low baseline fees for residential and nursing home care should not be ignorant of the possible outcomes of its actions.

The effectiveness of inspection procedures in identifying abuse appears to be limited; some inspectors believe that, irrespective of the quality of inspection, acts of abuse are only likely to come to light if one or more individuals (usually current or former members of staff) 'blow the whistle'. Similarly, although all SSDs are required to establish contractual arrangements with independent sector providers of residential and nursing home care, the robustness of contract monitoring arrangements appears to be limited, due to a combination of lack of experience in the monitoring process, lack of resources being directed towards the monitoring of contracts, and the difficulty of proving that practice standards in any given home are unacceptable. Therefore, regular inspection and/or contract monitoring appears unlikely to uncover most acts of abuse within homes.

DENYING ABUSE

There are a number of 'political' considerations which tend to encourage denial of the nature and extent of any abuse which may occur in local authority residential homes. SSDs are particularly sensitive to negative media coverage; it is clearly newsworthy if an organisation ostensibly devoted to the care of people fails to act in such a way as to secure that care – as is alleged in numerous cases of child abuse, for example, or in respect of the revelations of abuse of older people at Nye Bevan Lodge.

A major concern for many local authorities, therefore, is to manage media coverage to encourage positive images of the SSD and avoid negative images. There are pragmatic political reasons for this, rooted in the processes of local democracy. Negative publicity creates an image of the SSD as badly managed, incompetent and uncaring: a perception which makes elected councillors feel profoundly uncomfortable. That this can have beneficial effects is clear, as the organisation may seek to act in positive ways to transform the public and media perception of its performance. However, if the SSD wishes to avoid negative publicity at all costs, this could lead to a sense of complacency about practice standards or denial about the reality of practice in residential care homes.

There may be a number of consequences of this, three of which are examined here:

1. A refusal to accept that abuse is a possibility in residential care homes run by the SSD, leading to a radical reframing (either consciously or unconsciously) of abusive incidents into other more acceptable terms.
2. The SSD minimising or ignoring the extent of the abuse that has been discovered, for fear of the negative publicity which might be encouraged by greater openness.
3. An active attempt to cover up evidence of abuse, again to avoid the impact of bad publicity. (This would clearly be the most serious consequence.)

DIRECT FORMS OF ABUSE

The preceding sections have concentrated upon an examination of the ways in which SSDs may contribute to abuse of older people in residential care, either by creating a climate within which abuse can flourish, or by denying its existence and/or extent. This section focuses on the ways in which a SSD might directly contribute to such abuse.

Perhaps the most common example of such abuse concerns the Personal Expenses Allowance (PEA) of residents in independent sector residential or nursing homes. SSDs are required to ensure that each individual they admit to a residential or nursing home retains an element of their income as a PEA; this may not be taken into account even as part payment for more expensive accommodation (DoH, 1995, Annex H, para. 13). When independent sector care was funded mainly by the Department of Social Security (DSS), many residential and nursing homes charged residents an 'all-in' weekly fee which was somewhat higher than the basic DSS payment rate on the working assumption that homes would have access to the resident's PEA to supplement the basic payment of the DSS. This was a clear example of abuse as taking the resident's PEA effectively left them with little or no money for any personal needs.

There is now an expectation that SSDs police the problem more effectively, thereby denying residential and nursing homes access to residents' PEA as a contribution to the basic fees for the home. Homes have sought to oppose any such move, basing their campaign on a statement in the Charging for Residential Accommodation Guide (CRAG) that the PEA is the resident's own money, and it is for the resident to decide how this money should be spent (DoH, 1995). They have argued that this means that a resident should therefore be allowed to spend the PEA in any way that s/he wishes, including to help secure more expensive accommodation. SSDs have sought to resist this, arguing that:

1. CRAG states that the PEA must be left with the resident.
2. The PEA is intended to be used for items such as 'stationery, personal toiletries, treats and small presents for friends and relatives' (DoH, 1995).
3. While the local authority is responsible for the full cost of residential and nursing home accommodation, an individual may choose accommodation which is more expensive than the local authority would usually expect to pay only if a 'third party' is willing and able to pay the difference (DoH, 1992); the DoH has indicated that a resident may not act as her/his own 'third party' (DoH, 1995).

As the above brief summary indicates, this is a difficult debate on a subject with complex moral implications regarding the nature of choice and its limitations, where the legal position is presently unclear. While the argument continues unabated, and appears incapable of resolution either by government directive or local authority action, many residents are being deprived of the only cash which is intended for their personal use, with such individuals having a questionable degree of choice in the matter. In one large SSD, information on the possible scope and extent of this problem was recently accumulated. It was discovered that for 29.6% of all residents the placement had been made at a rate which was up to £13.00 higher than the rate which the SSD would usually expect to pay. It can be surmised (but not proved) that a high proportion of these residents are contributing all or part of their PEA, with scant lip-service paid to the principle of choice concerning its use, to pay for the basic cost of care.

The effect of this is clear; the particular SSD is failing to protect people from acts of direct financial abuse. The overall sums involved are massive; in the above SSD, it is estimated that almost £1m per annum is being contributed via third party payments to the cost of residential and nursing home care. The amount of this which originated from the residents' PEA is impossible to calculate precisely, but a conservative estimate might indicate that as much as £250,000 per annum is coming from this source. If other SSDs are facing the same difficulty in similar proportions, the national dimensions of this problem are immense. Given that those people in need of state funding for residential and nursing home care are amongst the most dependent in society, and arguably the least able to make an informed free choice, and that they have come to SSDs for care and assistance not exploitation, this situation is profoundly disturbing.

The closure of SSD-run residential homes, which is an increasingly common occurrence, also constitutes a form of abuse. No local authority takes such decisions lightly, but is often forced to it by a combination of:

- financial necessity;
- a policy preference for service users to be maintained in their own homes;
- over supply of residential beds due to unfettered independent sector expansion;
- government policy ensuring that it is cheaper for SSDs to purchase residential care from the independent sector than to continue with in-house services.

Regardless of these reasons, it could be predicted that the announcement in the local media of closures of what they termed 'old folks' homes' would receive critical coverage and may well lead to a vigorous campaign to keep them open. Underpinning such a campaign is an appeal to the 'caring' local authority not to close the home 'heartlessly' and thereby 'destroy' the lives of residents. A multi-layered message is therefore conveyed to both officers and councillors, the elements of which can be summarised as follows:

1. It is the responsibility of the SSD to care for people.
2. Closing a residential home is not the act of a caring SSD.
3. Residents' lives will be damaged as a result of the closure.
4. Negative publicity will result from this.
5. The people concerned, directly as residents or indirectly as family and friends, have votes and may exercise them in a particular way at the next local election.

It is difficult for a local authority to mount an effective rebuttal of any of the propositions listed above. However, in the context of this paper, the third point is critical: it could be argued that the lives of residents in homes which are to be closed are damaged in that their health suffers and the likelihood of death either just before or after any move is considerably increased. This impact can only be termed abusive. While SSDs may argue that no other decisions are possible and that the consequences are to be regretted, this does not in any way lessen the impact on residents and their families.

CONCLUSION

This paper has sought to address the specific involvement of local authorities in the abuse of people living in residential or nursing home care. It has focused on aspects of the way in which SSDs are organised which may create the climate for abuse, may seek to deny or minimise the existence of abuse, or which may be a form of direct abuse. In many cases, the difficult decisions forced on SSDs as they seek to balance apparently ever-reducing budgets should not be minimised. However, financial pressures should not be a pretext for failing to address the problems which have been identified, many, if not all, of which could be resolved at no extra cost to the budget, to the benefit of all those residents who are currently being abused. For SSDs to continue to have a moral justification for their central role in the management of community care, some remedial action is urgently required.

Ten

Setting and maintaining standards

George Mabon

INTRODUCTION

It is not my task to analyse 'abuse', but it will be helpful to make clear the position adopted in this chapter. It is that abuse is to hurting people as murder is to killing people. It is possible to kill people unintentionally; it is not possible to murder unintentionally. it is possible to hurt someone unintentionally, it is not possible to abuse someone unintentionally.

Informal soundings among home owners indicate that most do not see elder abuse as a pressing issue in their homes. Supervision, training, policies and procedures are thought to be so well developed that 'it couldn't happen here' was the common response. That is worrying.

This chapter will discuss setting and maintaining standards to deal with potential and actual abuse of older people in a context of promoting good practice in general. The perspective will be that of owners and managers of homes. It will look briefly at the notion of 'standards' and then, in relation to setting and maintaining them in residential settings, for older people, will try to answer four simple questions :

1. where do we start from?
2. what do we need to do to avoid or deal with the abuse of older people in residential settings?
3. how can we do it?
4. how can we sustain it?

STANDARDS

In everyday life the notion of standard relates closely to judgement, uprightness, comparison, measurement and achievement. We may disagree about what are high and low standards of behaviour, but most of us admit that they exist, and that they are important in giving us a framework against which to judge performance.

My mother is in her mid-eighties. She still lives on her own and looks after herself, as the song says, 'with a little help from her friends'. Her standards of hygiene in the kitchen are falling. Formally, they are much as they have always been. Actually, they have deteriorated simply because she cannot see the dirt as well as she did. Her established standards are not being maintained because she is incapable of judging adequately what she has done.

The mismatch between formal and actual standards is important in homes for older people. Formal standards are those written down, or, in the case of unwritten standards, those likely to be stated because they are professionally acceptable or match the prevailing orthodoxies. Actual standards can be deduced from observable behaviour. It may be necessary to observe and talk with staff, residents, relatives, other visitors and management to be sure of the actual standards operating in a home. So, for example, a home may state that residents may go to bed whenever they wish. Evening visits might show all communal rooms empty by 8.00 p.m., all residents tucked up in their own rooms and the staff busy with domestic work. Similarly, in relation to privacy, one of the home's standards may be that no member of staff will enter residents' rooms without their permission except in an emergency. Actually, staff breeze in and out with only the most perfunctory knock on the door.

The Social Services Inspectorate (SSI, 1990), and the Care Sector Consortium (1992) adopt fairly restrictive views of standards. The former claims that standards are criteria for judging quality, worth or value and that they must be validated, as explicit and precise as possible, justifiable and logically sound and practicable. In addition, they may be absolute or relative, objective or based on subjective judgement, tangible or intangible (SSI 1990 p3). The latter regards them as 'comprehensive yet precise descriptions of what people need to be able to do in the work environment, expressed in terms of the outcomes people are expected to achieve.' (Care Sector Consortium, 1992, pii) . Both are concerned to promote formal standards.

However, for managers, especially where they are also providers, it is not enough only to promote formal standards. One thing they cannot countenance is adherence to formal standards in their presence and reversion to some other in their absence. People cannot be free to work in the way they wish unless that way matches the home's formal standards. Only when there is a close match between formal and actual can management feel comfortable. That close match depends on people having the knowledge, skills, and above all, commitment, to follow the formal standards of the home.

WHERE DO WE START FROM?

No residential setting starts from scratch. Ranges of formal standards are set by a clutch of regulators from county and district councils. Every resident, and worker, at whatever level, has their own set, soaked up from diverse life experiences. Somehow they all have to be focused to create a distinctive life setting for those who live and work there.

It is a mistake to see the development of standards as an end in itself. Standards should be rooted in the philosophy of the home. They are instrumental, a means to the end of achieving aims and objectives. Those aims and objectives, however set originally, need to become the joint product of residents, staff and management so that life in homes is:

> a positive experience in which residents are enabled to do *more*, not less, with their lives; to exercise *more*, not less control and choice; to live in *dignity* and *privacy*; and to have their basic *human rights* safeguarded. (Wagner in HAFLI, 1989 p3)

Seeking to achieve that experience requires knowledge of a number of 'givens'. They include, among others, facts about residents, staff, staffing levels and staff training. We can do no more here than look at a sample of such facts from a fairly typical independent sector home as background to what follows. The home in question had twenty eight residents at the time this factual snapshot was taken. It should be seen as indicative rather than representative.

Residents

Residents are becoming older: fifty per cent are over ninety years old. Over fifty per cent take three or more prescribed drugs and

Figure 1

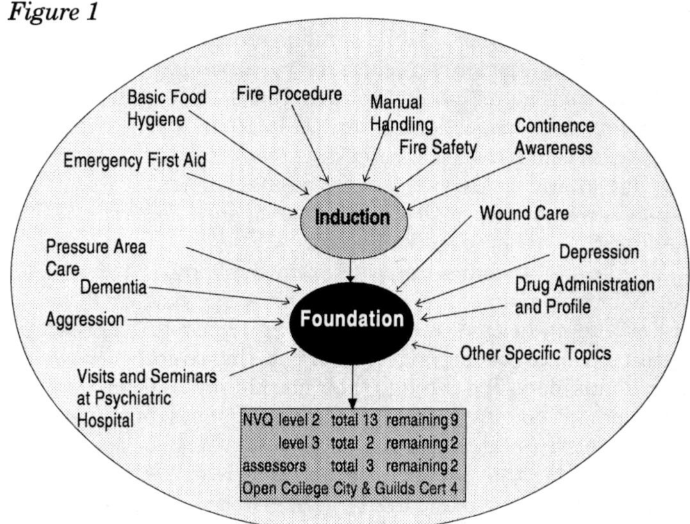

(Diagram and training material prepared by Mrs Katy Twyford, now with Hampshire Social Services Department Training Unit)

three residents take five or more. Less than half are able to dress themselves, only two can bath themselves and only eight climb stairs unaided.

Family and friends are far flung. Six residents see relatives once a year at most. Twelve see relatives or friends at least once per week, but six have less than six visits a year from friends or relatives and some have none. Match that with the level of frailty of the residents and the message about potential for abuse is strong.

Staff

Unfortunately, minimum staffing levels are not high. Hampshire's requirements are based on the provision of eleven daytime care hours per resident per week plus any additional hours required to ensure enough staff on the premises to ensure safety in emergencies. Management time is often included in the day time hours. Night cover is limited. Homes below ten residents need no one awake. For homes with from ten to twenty residents, the requirement is one staff member awake and one asleep, and for those from twenty one to thirty residents there are to be two staff awake rising in homes with above thirty residents to two staff awake and one asleep.

It is open to inspection units or managers to require or provide more staff as residents become more dependent. Experience suggests such adjustments are rare. Indeed, one result of open reporting of the inspections of the local authority's own homes is awareness that local authorities are sometimes not meeting the staffing standards they expect of the independent sector. That cannot give inspection units confidence in enforcing staffing standards in the independent sector.

The level of training undertaken in the home that has been taken as the example is indicated here. All new staff would undertake induction and foundation training. Thereafter, training would be arranged to meet the training needs of individuals identified through their normal supervision and staff development arrangements. In spite of equal opportunities policies, it is inevitable that short stay staff will not be adequately trained. Add to that the fact that in the private sector, and to a lesser degree elsewhere, most managers and proprietors are relatively unqualified in social care except through experience and it becomes obvious that there is not a good base on which to develop a sensitive approach to the recognition and avoidance of abuse.

WHAT DO WE NEED TO DO TO AVOID OR DEAL WITH THE ABUSE OF OLDER PEOPLE IN RESIDENTIAL SETTINGS?

We need to do many things. Here I shall look at only three: the need to accept that there is a potential or actual problem; the importance of seeing abuse of older people against the backdrop of general good practice aimed at helping residents maintain as much control as possible over their own lives; and the importance of good staff development and training.

First, we need to persuade managers and staff that there is a potential or actual problem relevant to them in their workplaces. Most simply do not believe it. Certainly few of the homes taking part in recent years in the Care Home of the Year competition run by *Care Weekly*, and even fewer of the associations and homes which make up United Care Associations, have policies, procedures or standards to deal with the abuse of older people. In addition, very few will have knowledge of material such as Jacki Pritchard's (1995) valuable training manual *The Abuse of Older People*. Virtually all, however, have in place statements of philosophy, aims and objectives, and policies and procedures designed to ensure that those aims and objectives are met. Yet it should be clear from the facts listed above about residents and staff that the potential for abuse is considerable. A combination of good luck, good management and well motivated, caring staff has so far avoided many serious problems.

In seeking to develop standards to avoid or deal with the abuse of older people in homes, we are effectively seeking to extend or focus existing practice. In Gerry Smale's (1992) terms, we are seeking to manage change. Perhaps the greatest change we should be seeking to bring about is to help older people in homes, people increasingly physically and mentally frail at entry, to control their own lives and maintain their rights.

That requires of us a logical commitment to the presumption that residents' wishes must be met unless there are publicly justifiable grounds for not meeting them. There can be no hiding behind a screen of alleged resident confusion or incompetence. Speaking of recent experience in Texas, Malcolm Holt (1995 pp2-23), said, 'the vulnerable adult is the primary client and will be presumed to be mentally competent to make decisions unless proven otherwise.' The burden of proof rests with those alleging incompetence. To be acceptable, that proof must be convincing to someone, resident or advocate, capable of evaluating it.

Morris (1994 p20), quotes from Reed and Wallercraft (1992), *A checklist on how workers can empower users*. Although originally for workers in mental health services, it would form a valuable part of foundation training for anyone providing care in residential settings. Its basic messages, freely transcribed, are put from the perspective of residents. These are set out below alongside examples of the kind of standards that could support them.

Message	**Possible Standard**
help us know our rights	on arrival we will provide you with a charter of rights, explain it to you and/or your friend and be prepared to go back to it whenever you wish.
relate to us as people, don't hide behind your professionalism	we will try always to respond to you and speak with you simply, without using technical words or jargon.

ask what we want and listen to our answers	we will try to provide what you want. If we cannot, we will tell you the reasons and, if you want, try to help you ask again in the right places.
treat our worries and complaints seriously	we will make sure you know as soon as possible what to do if you want to complain and will help you to get someone else to help if we cannot. If you think things are not being dealt with adequately we will help you take it further.
look at us with open eyes and help us to develop, maintain, or resurrect our skills and knowledge	we will work with you to help you do as much as possible for yourself, to get you as fit and mobile as we can. We will write down what we agree with you and change it only after discussion and agreement.
give us information and help us understand it	on arrival we will provide you with a handbook telling you all about what goes on in the home and a contract telling you what you can expect of us and we of you. We will work with you over time to help you understand it.
treat us as equals and recognise that you sometimes we want to be left alone	we will try always to remember that this is your home and that you have the same rights in your private room space as any householder. We will always address you politely by your chosen name and will not enter your room without your permission except in emergencies.
learn about us by talking with us	we will try to make sure we have time to talk with you, to learn what you want us to know about your past so that we may help you to a better future. We will treat everything you tell us as

confidential within the rules of the home

Abuse removes from older people substantial control of their own lives. Standards such as those roughed out above would go some way towards avoiding abuse. They are, however, insufficient. For example, a resident's room is his or her own personal space. A standard might state that 'staff will encourage residents to do within their rooms whatever they want, with whoever they want, within their capabilities, the law and the agreed rules of the home'. Management or staff who used a two way communication system to eavesdrop would be seriously abusing resident privacy. Standards need to be in place governing the use of such systems and encouraging staff to report malpractice with guaranteed management support. The 'Whistleblower Protection Bill', sponsored by Tony Wright MP, is unlikely to become law but is an indication of public concern.

Consideration here of staff development and training must be brief. It seems very few years since the proprietor of a home for over twenty residents said that his staff needed no training. They were, he said, middle aged women who had raised families and gained considerable life experience. That sits uneasily with Dick Clough's view that caring is a complex, physically difficult and stressful job for which good training is an essential prerequisite. (See Chapter 12.) Recently in Hampshire we mounted a series of courses on quality assurance and staff development. Evaluation by the owner and manager participants revealed a strong feeling of inadequacy about their general management skills. Many were convinced that without improving those skills they would find it difficult to implement staff development policies and training. It is worrying to see such feelings of inadequacy among management, one of whose most important functions is to see that the benefits of training in general, and NVQ awards in particular, which at least have standards related to abuse, are shared and maintained.

HOW CAN WE DO IT?

In addition to raising awareness through improving management competence, staff development and training with the aim that residents retain control of their own lives, there are at least three other inter-related possibilities.

First, local authority inspection departments, now impartially inspecting both local authority and independent provision, could, under Regulation 9 of the Registered Care Homes Regulations, 1984, require residential and dual registered home providers to develop and maintain policies, procedures and standards to deal with potential and actual abuse of older people in their care. No comparable regulation exists for nursing homes.

Secondly, local authority purchasing/commissioning sections might require homes to provide policies, procedures and standards as a condition of doing business. They already set requirements for equal opportunities and improper discrimination, so it would not be difficult to do the same to counter elder abuse.

Thirdly, provider trade/professional bodies might insist on such policies, procedures and standards as a condition of membership and back them with appropriate sanctions.

Providers will not find it easy to develop relevant standards. They will need help to pick their way through a number of documents. One possibility is for interested bodies to work together or separately to produce national draft guidance. Members of such a group might be: Action on Elder Abuse, The Residential Forum, Counsel and Care, the Heads of Inspection Units and the National Association of Inspection and Registration Officers (NAIRO) together with provider associations. It would almost certainly, however, be better to adopt an approach like that used in Hampshire to produce policies and procedures for *Avoiding Restraint in Residential Care for Older People*. A working group of local authority and independent sector providers or managers, the principal adviser, an occupational therapist with a keen interest in care planning and an inspector appointed jointly by social services and a district health authority, produced a policy framework supported by practice guides. It was then adopted by the local authority and the main trade/professional association and issued to all homes. Plans are now in place for a similar exercise on policies and procedures for dealing with potential and actual abuse of older people in residential care.

Perhaps the greatest weakness of the original piece of work was a failure adequately to involve residents and hands-on care staff in its development and implementation in homes. That weakness must be avoided this time. It will not be easy. Fortunately, user organisations and the Relatives Association are beginning to develop presence and strength and would have an important role to play.

HOW CAN WE SUSTAIN IT?

Standards to prevent or deal with the abuse of older people in residential care will not work if they are dependent largely on external enforcement. Inspection and registration units, commissioning/purchasing sections and trade/professional organisations are important but insufficient to maintain standards. They have the same kind of impact on providers as a police car in the slow lane of a motorway has on most motorists. The police car causes a sixty nine miles an hour traffic jam and the 'enforcers' tend to cause a flurry of activity around their visit which tails off rapidly when they are out of sight.

Standards to avoid or deal with abuse will work best where they are properly integrated into homes' general procedures and standards. They in turn should seek to promote the values outlined in 'Home Life' (1984), Wagner (1988), and Homes are for Living in (1989). There is additional exciting work underway through the Residential Forum and the Centre for Policy on Ageing to revisit the values inherent in 'Home Life' in the light of practice developments over the last ten years. The Residential Forum's efforts to produce standards with a very strong user perspective backed by a manager's manual to ensure ready translation into practice is a particularly interesting development. The first essential for maintaining standards then is a clear, shared philosophy of care for the home, informing well specified policies, procedures and standards designed to give maximum control to residents with the help of their front line staff.

Three other things would seem necessary if standards are to be sustained. The first is a move towards the principles of what Evans and Pottage (1992) described as 'The Competent Workplace'. Its shift to an organisational system in which front line staff link closely and take decisions with customers, has the benefit of removing the need felt by many managers to be constantly on the spot to make sure that the formal values of a command management system coincide with actual values and standards in the home.

The development of 'The Competent Workplace' relies heavily on the close involvement of staff and residents to change the culture of homes towards user focus and control. For that to work, education and training for management and staff is crucial. One of the outcomes of the Department of Health's 'Caring in Homes Initiative' was 'How to Manage Your Training' (Hillyard-Parker et al, 1993). It is aimed specifically at helping managers ensure quality in training that will guarantee quality in care. It would certainly help those Hampshire managers who felt relatively inadequate, though of itself is potentially mechanistic unless the home's philosophy is right.

The second is the development of a strong commitment to listen carefully to residents and workers and to act on what is said. Most quality assurance systems have some kind of feedback mechanism. *Inside Quality Assurance* (1991), also developed within the 'Caring in Homes Initiative', is probably unique in the degree of its focus on users, staff and relatives to find out what the place feels like to live in and what needs to be done to improve it. A very simple instrument developed by Chris Payne (1994) with providers in North Tyneside *Evaluating the Quality of Care: A Self Assessment Manual*, is especially useful in involving staff in thoughtful review of practice in their workplace. Those, coupled with a quality assurance system demanding regular reviews of the home's systems, policies, procedures and standards, would do much to maintain standards.

The final component is really part of a quality assurance system, but so important it is worth separate attention. Any home seeking to maintain standards needs an efficient, easy to use, complaints and comments system. Simply to write a couple of paragraphs into a contract or brochure is inadequate. Residents and staff need to feel comfortable about complaining and asking for, or suggesting, changes in their homes. The package of materials, audio, video and written, produced by EBS Trust (1994), 'Some Like It Hotter', is a useful tool to promote and encourage complaint and comment.

CONCLUSION

To avoid the dangers of abuse, homes need to have their basic values, aims and objectives, policies and procedures right and in shared ownership. Among those policies and procedures and related standards should be those specifically related to the abuse of older people in residential care.

Success in care would then revolve around residents maintaining maximum control of their own lives in a home where actual values and those formally agreed between residents, staff and providers are closely matched and monitored so that people can live and work largely as they wish.

Part Four:

Suspicions, Allegations and Action

Eleven

Blowing the whistle on elder abuse

Jill Manthorpe

This chapter draws attention to two distinct debates, the first covering what has become known as whistle-blowing and the second to the discovery and disclosure processes involved in combating or preventing elder abuse. It focuses on the interface between the two - that is the dilemmas involved when cases of suspected abuse of vulnerable adults are revealed by employees of the organisation concerned to the outside world. Such dilemmas raise important issues for us all because they test the notions of accountability, professionalism and loyalty. Nonetheless they are not new issues and the history of long-term care shows that a number of individuals have had to face the dilemmas described in this chapter (see Martin, 1985).

THE WHISTLE-BLOWING CONTEXT

The formation of the concept of whistle-blowing is not confined to welfare services. It is a concept with its roots in industry as well. The essential elements of whistle-blowing involve an employee who, dissatisfied with his or her organisation's behaviour, independently reports it to an outside agency, such as the press, a trade union, professional body, elected representative or an organisational regulator. To do so has its costs, as the employee may be breaking explicit instructions or implicit expectations of loyalty and confidence. The direct costs may include dismissal, stress, and problems obtaining future employment.

Hunt (1995, p.1) comments that a whistle-blower is 'half

trouble-maker, half hero' and draws attention to the immediate political context to explain why whistle-blowing has achieved a certain public prominence. He ascribes this to a crisis of legitimacy:

> Whistle blowing occurs at the unsettling intersection of an increasingly generalised allegiance to personal autonomy, and civil and human rights, and the decreasing public accountability of our institutions. (p. xiv)

Hunt's work is concentrated on the British National Health Service and he sees whistle-blowing as the potential response of many employees who are concerned at the development of commercial or industrial models inside a previously professionally dominated service. He argues that principles such as confidentiality have been subtly altered from protection of patients to the protection of valuable commercial information or the protection of an organisation's reputation or public relations image.

It is as if Hunt sees whistle blowing as a sort of fault - line, marking the clash between two distinct continental masses: the first based on professional ethics and the second resting on commercial models. In the personal social services this is typified by the purchaser : provider split of the reformed NHS under the NHS and Community Care Act 1990 and the greater concentration within the NHS on efficiency and market principles. The debate over whistle-blowing however is not confined to the NHS although many of the best known public examples are from this sphere. Hunt (1995) discusses the cases of Graham Pink, Helen Zeitlin and Chris Chapman. There are close links to industrial and commercial concerns and other service providers. Dr Tony Wright, MP, a sponsor of a bill to protect whistle-blowers from reprisals referred to the Lyme Regis canoeing accident in 1994. (See Guardian, 28 June 1995, p.9). Derek Fatchett, another of the bill's sponsors referred to the Piper Alpha oil platform disaster.

A recent example outside the NHS but in a health setting concerns the case of Rosa Arnold who was dismissed as matron of a nursing home and was awarded £10,000 by an industrial tribunal who upheld her claim of unfair dismissal. Arnold voiced her concerns to her employers and the nursing homes' inspectorate. She was particularly aware of her duty under the nursing code of professional conduct and is reported as noting the inspectorate had 'no clout' (Cassidy, 1995).

In contrast, accountability for those who are not professionally trained is less easy to maintain as an abstract commitment to users unless wider notions of humanity and moral criteria are considered. As Beardshaw (1981) notes:

> A primitive reluctance to 'rat' or 'sneak' on friends and colleagues is linked in most employees' minds with loyalty to the body that employs them - plus a healthy fear of being sacked without a pension or a reference. (p.3)

Such discussions widen the debate from a focus on the individual whistle-blower who reports an incident to the observational system. It is clearly related to another debate that is taking place in both the welfare and commercial worlds, that of risk management. Whether a person sees him or herself as a whistle-blower is a product or how he or she anticipates his or her behaviour will be seen by the organisation, managers and colleagues. It may be useful to look at three organisational typologies to see whether they relate to the creation of the whistle-blowing identity.

CONSTRUCTING THE WHISTLE-BLOWER

Within health and welfare organisations decisions have traditionally been made by professionals, entrusted with the management of their organisations because of their expert knowledge, experience and judgement. Disagreement has been tolerated and is possible because there has been a large degree of autonomy, mutual trust and discretion. Hood et al (1992) have explored how organisations make decisions and respond to situations of uncertainty and this has been extended by Alaszewski and Walsh (1995) who note three relevant classifications:

- Blaming or learning
- Anticipating or responding
- Expert or public involvement

These need some clarification and linking with the theme of abuse.

Some organisations allocate responsibility or blame to certain individuals who are deemed to be at fault. This approach resonates with the 'bad apple' theory of whistle-blowing, a theory which Hunt declares to be untenable. He notes that the scenario of a 'good' whistle-blower who reveals a 'bad' (and atypical) practice or member of an organisation and then (despite initial difficulties) is proved right, is simplistic. Indeed the whistle-blower may be blamed and Hunt lists the possible reactions to whistle-blowing ranging from organisational isolation to redundancy, disciplinary procedures and personal vilification (1995, pp.155-158). Even where a whistle-blower is seen to have been correct, a blaming organisation may find it difficult to trust an employee who has breached a culture of organisational loyalty. Equally a blaming organisation may maintain that removing the 'bad apple' is an adequate response, with no real investigation of the system that allowed a 'bad apple' to survive.

The converse type is a learning organisation, where details of mistakes or misgivings about organisational practices are encouraged in a climate of learning and 'no fault' responses. Mistakes are not hidden but are seen as an opportunity to review procedures in a confidential no-blame reporting system. Employee hot lines have been given as good examples of such systems, or the confidential systems applying to air-line pilots 'near misses' or the national system of confidential enquiries into maternal deaths (Cloake, 1989). Such practices emphasise that an organisation will make no recriminations and encourage internal discussion, rather than efforts at covering up, and thus making matters worse. The role of whistle-blower ideally becomes redundant because learning organisations want to know what is wrong and aim to correct it.

The second area covers organisations' behaviour in relation to predicting and anticipating problems. Such organisations try to build up systems of checks and counter-checks to ensure consumer or client safety. In terms of residential care for older people, for example, such an organisation would weave a complicated set of quality measures, internally and externally monitored, based on research findings about certain risk factors for bad practice, neglect or abuse. It would be secure and confident in its staff and procedures. Whistle-blowing would represent a fundamental challenge to such an organisation since it would reveal that its internal measures were not adequate and would conflict with its public image of certainty and coherence. In welfare services this approach is flawed since we have no real scientific basis on which to rely with any certainty. We have suggestions, for example, of possible risk factors in relation to elder abuse at both domestic and institutional levels (see Clough, 1994), but we do not yet have certainty in this area, if indeed that is ever possible.

Prediction then has its limits in elder abuse, as in many other human services areas, so it may be that organisations develop resilience: that is they develop systems for early identification of and rapid response to such problems. Thus if an allegation of bad practice or abuse is made, certain procedures are put into place. The development of policy guidelines, protocols and practice guidance can be usefully seen in this context. Their unifying characteristics lie in their attempts to standardise procedures so that responses to allegations or suspicions are uniform and that response times are given in line with certain established priorities. Efforts are made in the development of such procedures to set out the nature of collaboration with other agencies. If we see elder abuse procedures in such light it becomes possible to explain why they are reactive and have had little to say about prevention or therapeutic services for individuals after the abuse has been discovered or confirmed.

The final relevant 'doctrinal contest', as Hood et al. (1992) term it, or organisational style, lies in the area of expert or public participation. Again this has clear relevance to the issue of whistle-blowing in areas such as elder abuse. A narrow view of human services would argue that such organisations are accountable to their share holders (in the case of commercial providers), Boards of Management and their electoral process (in the case of voluntary organisations and charities) or to elected members and their electorate (in the case of local authority social services providers). We need to appreciate though that in the case of small, private residential homes accountability is less easy to determine as many owners manage family-run concerns. Here they may carry a very real form of personal financial liability as well as personal or professional reputation; however, there may well be limited accountability outside the regulatory framework of inspection or care management monitoring, if appropriate.

In terms of day-to-day management of larger homes, a professional and hierarchical model may operate, with trust placed in the superior expert view of a medical practitioner or senior nurse. Such a view is not without a certain logic. It is clear where responsibility lies and doctors, for example, are subject to professional codes of ethics and the powers of their self-regulating professional bodies. Alaszewski and Manthorpe, (1995), discuss Durkheim's explanations for this. Indeed many older people in particular appear very supportive of the idea of medical expertise, that is that the doctor or matron knows best. They may support their views on the use of restraint, for instance, or on decisions to admit people to hospital or long-term care. Whistle-blowing is possible in this area when experts disagree with each other on fundamental issues, such as moral criteria or values. However some experts would place each others' different work practices as outside their responsibility, and therefore take no action even when concerned.

In contrast a broad view of participation is more diffuse. It reveals the inconsistencies and 'grey areas' around ethical or moral issues or even around what constitutes quality or good practice. Pluralistic evaluation, for example, shows that there are many different versions of success and that different perspectives may place different values on services (see Smith and Cantley, 1985). In the area of elder abuse a long standing debate continues about the definition of such a phenomenon, with different experts discussing their views of what constitutes abuse and, indeed, whether the term is helpful or accurate. In the United States this debate has been largely confined to medical and social work professionals or academics. By contrast, in the UK a more participationist view of the definition of elder abuse has evolved with Action on Elder Abuse consulting its members and interested organisations about the definition (see Action on Elder Abuse Bulletin, 1994). In relation to the inspection of residential care services we can discern a move towards a broader involvement in establishing and monitoring standards. These may undercut the need for whistle-blowing.

Compare, for example, the peer system of inspection in the Health Advisory Service whereby fellow professionals, on secondment and not part of an established inspectorate, use their professional experience to deal with individual practice with the Independent Inspection Units, distanced though not separate, from local authority social services departments under the NHS and Community Care Act 1990 (Day and Klein, 1990). The latter's role has been augmented by lay inspection, whereby members of the public are invited to offer a 'lay' perspective to ground the professional judgement in what is publicly acceptable (see Clough, 1994). Both systems have the potential to contribute to debates on elder abuse and it is interesting, with benefit of hindsight, to see how frequently the Health Advisory Service (HAS) refer to practices several people might term abusive rather than less than ideal practice. For example, Day and Klein found 26 of 35 HAS reports on services for older people identified the use of restraints as an issue for concern (p. 10), while 17 out of 35 referred to custodial ward routines.

Hood and colleague's work on organisational typologies can be extended to cover the way decisions are made at a variety of levels. We can see that employees' willingness to complain externally about issues at work is not simply related to their strength of feeling or development of a sense of morality; it is bound up with the identity and the practices of the employing organisation, whether it is in the public or private sector. In the next section I move to discuss common features of dealing with the issues of confidentiality and anonymity in relation to elder abuse and neglect. Many cases of elder abuse have involved an element of whistle-blowing; it is appropriate to bring the debates together.

ACTING ON ELDER ABUSE

Both whistle-blowing and elder abuse entered the public domain, becoming highly visible issues for professionals working with older people, in the 1980s. The case of Graham Pink (summarised in Pilgrim, 1995, p. 79-80), for example, involved a hospital charge nurse who reported to a newspaper his concerns about the standard of care in his hospital and was dismissed (*Guardian*, 1990). Numerous publications, training courses and conferences have raised professional and policy makers' attention to the existence of elder abuse, though as other contributors to this book have suggested the preliminary focus has been on abuse in domestic settings (see Frank Glendenning Chapter Four).

The common features concern the role and accountability of the employee, particularly when an employee is also a professional, together with a growing interest in consumer rights and the balance of power between purchasers and providers. The particular vulnerable position of those who receive services from welfare services, regardless of payment arrangements, sources of funding or status of the service provider makes elder abuse an important issue for those receiving and providing residential and nursing home care.

ACCOUNTABILITY

The role and accountability of employees clearly distinguishes whistle-blowers from those who are concerned on behalf of others on the basis of other relationships. A watchdog role, for example, may be the clear purpose of a voluntary organisation or an association of relatives. Employees, however, owe certain duties to the employer and indeed duties to their patients, clients or service users. Action on Elder Abuse (1994) advises care home staff to report their concerns despite their possible fear of repercussions:

> People are often worried about 'rocking the boat' and may not know who to turn to or how to deal with the situation. It is important that you do tell someone what is happening. The older person concerned may not be able to raise the alarm themselves, and the situation may continue or get even worse if you do not pass on what you know.

It notes that enquiries to Public Concern at Work a free legal advice centre can be made anonymously. Public Concern at Work (1995) also advises individuals that they can talk to them 'without breaking any term in your employment contract or any duty of confidence or loyalty you owe your employer ... in most cases it is best to discuss the concern with us before you raise it'.

Alternatively professionals may find their own associations helpful. The British Association of Social Workers (BASW), for example, produced its own code of practice on whistle-blowing in 1993.

Some employers indeed encourage such moves. According to a recent report, a NHS Trust (Horizon) is encouraging staff to contact the charity Public Concern at Work.

We see here an acknowledgement that many employees working in residential or day care services are fearful of losing their jobs on the basis of being seen as trouble-makers. They may be vulnerable because they have generally limited qualifications and work in areas where employment is hard to find. Lee-Trewick (1994) describes the work of nursing/home staff and notes how staff were often women, working locally and on a part-time basis.

Indeed, as the experience of Dick Clough in this volume (Chapter 12) suggests, whistle-blowers have often been involved in trying to bring to attention practices they have found abusive or suspicious because they felt accountable in vague rather than precise forms. In those cases he has investigated where abuse was not reported he ascribes this to new staff not always being aware that particular practices are wrong. Alternatively he suggests that the persistent hiding of poor practice is because people feel they cannot 'blow the gaff on their mates'. People then may feel accountable - but to their colleagues rather than to users. The impact of organisational culture was brought out in the enquiry held into allegations made by another whistle-blower, Susan Machin, a social worker employed at Ashworth Special Hospital, a secure psychiatric hospital (Blom-Cooper, 1992). Machin was dismissed in 1994 but won an industrial tribunal in 1995; the case prompting the deputy chairperson of the British Association of Social Workers to say:

> We have to produce a climate where institutions are less defensive about criticism and we must create better rights for whistle-blowers (*Community Care* 1995, p.3)

Although this context did not involve older people per se as Ashworth's patients cover a broad age span, it is important in reminding us that dehumanising practices existed because nurses and patients were disempowered ; the nurses' professional sense of accountability was not developed by their education or training, nor assisted by professional guidance, protocols, role models, supervision nor mentorship (Dale, Rae and Tarbuck, 1995).

Nevertheless, this case includes some optimistic features, for as Potier and Ghosh (1995) point out, reaction to whistleblowers was complex. Problems over accountability have a long history. Barton, in his foreword to the campaigning document *Sans Everything*, (Robb, 1967) a powerful critique of long-term hospital provision for older people, noted:

> Staff of institutions develop neurotic self-propagating traditions such as misplaced loyalty of one staff member to another. Only a deviant will shop a colleague ... Victimisation of anyone who is critical, whether justifiable or not, may be automatic. (p.x).

It is interesting to note that Robb's collected evidence for *Sans Everything: A Case to Answer* (1967) was mostly given in response to a letter to *The Times* and represented 'hundreds of letters' according to Robb (1967, pxiii). She guaranteed the authors confidentiality and placed their sworn affidavits with solicitors; clearly whistle-blowing was perceived as potentially dangerous.

Sans Everything puts the explanation for abuse in the context of hospitals and their professional hierarchies. Nurses, it is argued, are unwilling and unable to challenge doctors, their own superiors or hospital management. The individual testimonies and Robb's own account of the admission of a Miss Willis to a mental hospital until released to a retirement home, are very much directed to the systems operating in a context of poor resources, demoralisation, service inadequacy and cultures of neglect and dehumanising practices.

Much of the doctors' testimonies, included as commentaries in *Sans Everything* stress the impact of overcrowding and poor practice. They note particularly the 'dumping' of older people in mental hospitals which was the real focus of the AEGIS enquiry (Aid for the Elderly in Government Institutions). There are several complex themes in this book relevant to abuse in residential settings some thirty years later, despite the closure of geriatric and psychogeriatric long-stay hospital provision (Darton and Wright, 1993).

Older people with significant disabilities are now to be found in nursing homes and residential care homes. Such provision may be organised around medical hierarchies where the use of the term 'Matron' is now mainly to be found. Indeed, residential care itself still often has a stigmatising and negative image (see Wagner 1988).

Nonetheless the systems surrounding mental health and community care have changed, with a far greater openness extending to official entrances and exits to the system as well as internal and external inspection. Abel-Smith's proposal for a Hospital or Health Service Commissioner, for example, along the lines of the then recently inaugurated Parliamentary Commissioner (known as the Ombudsman) was implemented, albeit for the NHS alone (Robb, 1967, p.134). Lessons from today's whistle-blowers need to be analysed to develop contemporary mechanisms to facilitate further safety nets to protect vulnerable older people, no matter the setting. The next section considers possible developments.

LISTENING EARLIER TO THE WHISTLE

There are signs that some authorities are accepting that it is in their own interest to develop a clear policy in relation to whistle-blowing. The London Borough of Southwark, for example, in a policy document circulated to all staff expects staff to raise concerns about care practice with their managers but recognises this can sometimes be difficult (Southwark, 1995). It gives alternative routes for staff to report their concerns and gives them an assurance they will not be victimised in the process.

There is an expectation that staff will follow internal procedures but the Department notes that some staff may feel anxious about reporting concerns and advises them to contact certain voluntary sector organisations which will take up the issue and keep the whistle-blower informed of what is happening. The document advises: 'You can talk to them about your situation at work to help ensure there are no reprisals or victimisation.'

In this way the notion of whistle-blowing has been taken up by an authority which has developed a system for supporting the individual. The London Borough of Lambeth also has plans to introduce a whistle-blowers' charter for its social services department and sheltered housing service, (Care Weekly, 1995), although this appears currently contentious.

Some might argue however that such moves are still inadequate. Furthermore, the private member's Whistle-blower's Protection Bill, sponsored by Tony Wright, MP., has also been criticised for insufficient protection (see *Care Weekly*, 1995). An alternative proposal for legal reform is to extend the Employment Protection Consolidation Act. This might lift the restriction on period of employment before unfair dismissal can be claimed and might remove the ceiling on compensation (see Stone, 1995).

However as such employer's policies in welfare services are recent developments it would be useful to have this work evaluated; such organisations seems on paper to be moving towards the 'learning model' identified earlier. It is, of course relatively easy to have such a policy on paper but such a commitment deserves to be valued and encouraged.

MANDATORY REPORTING

Mandatory reporting, a feature of some US States' procedures has not been widely taken up in the UK. It makes it compulsory for human service workers to report suspicions of abuse or face penalties. Where it is discussed is in the context of breaking professional trust with carers at domestic level, such as a community nurse reporting a stressed carer for suspected abuse (e.g. Manthorpe, 1993). Mandatory reporting however needs to be considered in the context of non-domestic abuse since legal obligations (and penalties for not obeying) are common in the US. They offer potential whistle-blowers added compulsion (through self-interest) to report abuse and offer them protection from employers' recriminations.

The arguments for mandatory reporting are summarised by

Quinn and Tomita (1986). They note that many US States have passed laws relating to mandatory reporting which provide immunity to those reporting suspected abuse or neglect. As a response, staff training on abuse has increased and there are increased referrals, even where no complaint has come forward. However they also point to possible dangers in such laws, noting that mandatory reporting does not guarantee appropriate intervention. Indeed the professional investigation may exacerbate the problem. Furthermore:

> Some physicians say that a client will not return for much-needed services if she learns that her physician must report her abusive situation, sometimes against her wishes (p.231).
>
> Such laws may also be seen as ageist or restrictive and they tend to concentrate on physical abuse and neglect (p.262).

Early debates on elder abuse have, not surprisingly, focused on the potential to reform the legal framework to provide for greater protection. Broadening the focus from an individualistic perspective on the possible 'victim' of abuse and the 'perpetrator' may help to develop the debate. Legal reform to protect whistle-blowers has some support and has the advantage of not being concentrated on care. It is built on the principles of employees' duties being more extensive than simply to their employers, for instance, to the environment or to the public. Recipients of care are included as citizens in these principles, deserving of specific rights because of their vulnerabilities, but also because they are consumers of a service.

Further approaches might include specific developments around care, namely increased proactive work by inspectorates to encourage complaints from any source. Many inspectorates make efforts to talk with care home residents in a confidential setting and many act on anonymous information. The development of Action of Elder Abuse's free-phone helpline may provide us with valuable information about callers who are employees and what they feel are inhabiting factors in resolving issues at work. However, as we have seen there are great continuities in the reasons outlined by Robb's report (1967) and cases from the 1990s (Hunt, 1995).

CONCLUSION

Whistle-blowing by employees is not a recent phenomenon. It appears in organisations that are defensive and which blame trouble-makers as well as poor practitioners. Such organisations work in the short-term and perhaps believe they have infallible systems of checks and supervision. They give high value to the opinion of experts even though these might disagree with each other or relationships deteriorate.

For older people in residential or nursing home care whistle-blowers offer a form of safety-net, but are highly unpredictable since staff may feel their loyalty to each other outweighs their duties to residents. Some staff may leave rather than face the dilemmas of deciding between their colleagues or residents. High staff turn-over is therefore a potentially interesting subject for inspectors.

Whistle-blowing may be the last resort of the frustrated and angry employee. In such circumstances evidence may be confusing and contradictory. At times, of course, false and malicious allegations may be made. Lessons from enquiry reports, however, reveal that whistle-blowers deserve to be listened to for such allegations have often been made initially and not upheld. In this area, inspectorates, service purchasers, service providers and policy-makers would be well advised to develop policies that undercut the need for whistle-blowing rather than facing the horror of each revelation and investigation afresh.

Twelve

Uncovering abuse

Dick Clough

This chapter focuses on uncovering abuse. It is one of the few occasions when Roger Clough and I have had material published on the same text, though we have known one another for many years. On occasions people have confused one of us for the other and I have taken great glory in the fact that people have said all sorts of nice things about the wonderful things that I have written which have, of course, been written by him. There is a link between Roger and me in the content of this chapter. Understandably, and properly, people prepare for occasions when they have to appear before an investigation. A witness in an enquiry which I undertook arrived with all sorts of books and reports. And not ten minutes into his presentation he said to me: 'Of course, Mr. Clough, I have been immensely impressed with all that you've written'. Even at the risk of demolishing a witness, I had to advise him that none of the books that he had in front of him had been written by me.

It has never ceased to amaze me that, as someone whose prime responsibility in employment terms is the promotion of good practice in social care in general and residential care in particular, I seem, more than most, to have looked at the seedier side of our work. People often ask me: 'How do you feel during enquiries?'. The answer is 'Usually quite depressed'. I try not to show it. But it is important to recognise that the people undertaking investigations are affected by what they see, hear and read. It is terribly hard in a service that one is usually proud to represent and proud to serve, to suddenly find yourself sitting in what I can only describe as a mass of dirt.

Let me move on to the processes which lead up to me or others being asked to undertake an enquiry. It needs to be said right at the outset that the enquiries are likely to be in a local government setting. It is local government that usually has to take the responsibility if ministers demand that there will be an enquiry. Indeed, central government rarely puts on enquiries any more; it orders local authorities to do so and local authorities have to pay. The expenses will vary with the numbers of people who sit, the length of time they take and the fees charged by individuals. More recently, there have been a number of examples where local government has stepped in first and actually called the enquiry.

Enquiries are traumatic experiences for all involved; there is no escape from that. And that is the reason why I have given a lot of thought to how they should be carried out. Remember that, if an enquiry is to be called, one usually finds that there have been one incident or a number of incidents of a particularly serious nature. The events may have taken place over a long time and involve more than one residential establishment and, in local government, may pervade a whole department. Indeed, there have been occasions when I have been asked to include in my brief a study of the Director of Social Services' role or even, in one case, that of the Metropolitan Police. Those sort of investigations are forcible reminders of the potential repercussions for the investigator!

One of the consequences of producing this paper is that I have had to continue to reflect on how I work and that I take the risk of declaring my strategy. Very early on I want to get hold of all the paper work and quickly to examine it. But as well, I want to get the feel of either the establishment itself, or the department itself.

I seek to reach a reasonable professional opinion based on the balance of probabilities. I do not seek absolute proof of the issues before me. There are two recurring themes:

- the first is the power of staff at all levels
- secondly, there is the management of those staff.

You will never escape from looking at those two issues for the reason that they are central to whether residential care is undertaken properly or not. For too many years I have stressed the significance of the power of staff and of the ease with which it can be abused. Of course, used properly such power can be advantageous to all involved. The most powerful people in any residential home for elderly people are the care assistants. Care assistants themselves may deny this. Many other people in residential services will deny it. But ask a 90 year old, frail elderly person as she is being toileted who is the most powerful person in her life at that time, and I have no doubt whom she will say. Care assistants are involved in the most private acts, sometimes the most undignified acts, the most personal acts with which we can expect any other person who is not a relative to be involved. They have control at any given time over other people's lives. And that must never ever be forgotten. Yet often we are too scared to send that message out to care assistants. Some managers and heads of units are reluctant to recognise either the importance or the power of care staff. This is not to deny that, in a different way, the head of a unit is also extremely powerful.

Indeed I rate management so important that I shall digress from the central thrust of this chapter to make a few points. The management of an establishment, be it the management of the unit itself or the management at a distance, is crucial. I have never ever understood why someone who is competent at running and managing on a day to day basis one residential care home, is thought automatically to be deemed to be competent to run twenty. The management technique, as a core may well be the same, but the technique will be so different. There are a number of really good heads of individual homes whose skills have been lost as they get absorbed into worrying about matters other than care, perhaps whether boilers are working, or a potential strike is to take place. many people train, get qualified and, as soon as they have their piece of paper, quit. No wonder management frequently is in turmoil.

If the head of the organisation does not value the provision of residential care, then there is little hope that the care itself will be of a high quality. If directors of social work or social services do not believe in residential care as a method of care, then it has virtually no chance of succeeding. There are many directors who do not believe in residential care as a method and, therefore, they should not see it practised in their authority. If you can't do residential care well, please don't do it at all. Residential care done badly is far worse than residential care not done at all.

What I have called a 'digression' allows me to make two points:

- the first is that investigators have values;
- the second is that I take careful account of the extent to which the heads of organisations value residential care.

They are elements towards which I am influenced in any enquiry.

The terms of reference for an enquiry are laid down by the commissioning agent, usually the local authority; if the Secretary of State or the Minister for Health has been involved, the terms will have to be approved also at that level. Usually they are wide and bland enough to allow me to do anything I consider to be appropriate and professional. As someone leading an enquiry, I can usually have an influence on the terms of reference.

Having been appointed, I need to examine the way to tackle the investigation. Recently I have taken to sitting alone, a fact of which some of my colleagues who also undertake enquiries have not always approved. There are a number of advantages to sitting alone. The first is in the way I conduct enquiries and conduct interviews and take evidence: I prefer that to be on a confidential, one-to-one basis. If I have a room full of people sitting with me, it is not easy for the likes of care assistants to talk. If the witness requires to be accompanied, then for obvious reasons I too would have to be. In a recent enquiry of the 56 people that I saw, only 5 chose to be accompanied. I don't have a note taker. I take my own notes. But I have been known on occasions actually to put the note book aside when people have been in such a state that it would be really quite wrong not to concentrate solely on them, ensuring that I write up the interview later. Sitting alone allows enquiries to be undertaken in much less time and, consequently, much less cost.

In taking the evidence, one needs to try and establish a rapport and a confidence quickly. There is always a presumption in any of these enquiries that some city slicker in a pin striped suit is going to appear and talk terribly posh and frighten the life out of people. Well I may frighten the life out of people on occasions, but I certainly do not talk 'terribly posh'.

There have been numerous occasions when people, particularly relatives and service users, have told me, 'This is our last chance; you are our last hope'. Now that really does frighten me. However, the nature of the calling of an enquiry means that events have reached a critical stage where some people will be very worried: 'What do we do next? Where can we go? No-one believes us'. Someone usually will have blown the whistle. Looking back over the many enquiries that I have now done, it has been interesting to consider who actually has blown the whistle. Interestingly on one occasion, it was the inspection and registration department who, having missed something in the first instance, certainly found it on a second visit. That was in a local authority home.

Whistle blowing picks up on the twin themes of the power base and fear. I am at a loss for words when trying to imagine how it is that people who clearly and blatantly are decent people watch and let poor practice continue. There seem three central reasons. The first is that they are frightened. Secondly, is the view that it is not the done thing to tell on your mate; constantly it happens that 'not wanting to blow the gaff on your mate' hides poor practice, a fact about which I get very angry. The third element is the uncertainty of newly appointed staff about their views. Thus, new staff with a bit of common sense come in, see something that does not appear to be right and do not trust their own judgement: 'These people have been here for ten or fifteen years. They've far more experience than me; they must be right. I'd better not say anything.'

An example of this occurred in the second enquiry I carried out. It was in a London borough in a local authority child care establishment where on this occasion I was sitting with a barrister. Four very junior members of staff noticed for months brown paper parcels coming into the establishment from Scandinavia, thought it was funny, and wondered about it. Eventually their concern got the better of them and they went off to the town hall and just simply said, 'We're worried; there are these packages arriving and we think there's something not right'. They were sent away with a flea in their ear. Some ten years later the head of that home who was receiving the packages was jailed for four years for offences involving pornographic literature and children. In the enquiry, we advertised in the national press and we got those four people back all able to testify that they had not known what was happening, but they felt something was wrong. There was no scrap of evidence in that department to say those people had ever been to the management in that authority , and each manager that we saw could not remember ever seeing them.

In circumstances like that it may not be surprising that I begin to get a bit frustrated. The frustration is on account of service users, relatives and those young staff. The message is clear: if we do not listen, no matter how silly the complaint may seem, something major will be missed. There are improvements: people are getting better at listening and some of the complaints procedures that have developed are good. On the other hand, at the other end of the scale, some complaints procedures are positively Draconian and are serving residential work poorly. Fear of what happens when allegations are made against staff is one of the reasons why people do not necessarily blow the gaff.

Indeed, I would contend that local authorities are suspension mad. Some actions smack of the most appalling justice on occasions. Constantly, I am told when I appear at an enquiry that the fact of people having been suspended is not a presumption of guilt: the process of suspension is nothing whatsoever to do with reaching an opinion on the case. To which I reply, 'You tell that to the person who's just been suspended'. I do not deny that there are certain cases when the authority has no choice but to suspend a staff member. But in my other role as General Secretary of the Social Care Association, I am appalled at what I learn of the way people have been treated from the moment an allegation is made. I am horrified at the number of occasions when people have been totally cleared in an investigation into an allegation but have not been able to go back to the establishment in which they work. The mud sticks. I need to be aware of this in conducting an enquiry.

There is also the matter of the time that it takes both for enquiries to be completed and for agencies to conclude their own actions. An enquiry that I undertook was completed in less than ten weeks at the request of the authority. For want of a better expression, I made a finding of guilt against those accused. The local disciplinary action against them did not start until seven months later. An earlier enquiry in a London borough had disciplinary action being taken against a member of staff eighteen months after my recommendations. Of course I am aware also that enquiries may take an inordinate amount of time, with people's lives and livelihood likely to be dependent on the outcome. Being able to set dates for an enquiry rapidly is a further reason why I prefer to sit alone. However, the fact of sitting alone raises important questions about personal power and the potential for abuse.

So there is a dilemma. On the one hand we must put service users first. I have never ever wanted to deny that. But when I face an audience, as I did last year, and am told that the child must always be believed, I have to ask: 'Is that then at the expense that the staff must never be believed?' I was told that in these circumstances staff had no rights. I will not operate in a world like that. Everyone has rights. If staff abuse residents in a residential home for elderly people, in the context of the people who are the subject of this book, then I shall be the first to demand that action is taken against them. Yet we must not forget the rights of staff.

It is worth reflecting on the nature of the abuse that is the subject of discussion. I think that in residential homes for elderly people, verbal abuse is more prevalent than physical abuse. In many ways, verbal abuse can be more violent as far as the recipient is concerned than any other form of abuse. This fact is difficult to bring home to the staff who are the front line workers, or face workers, with residents. Earlier I have stressed both their importance and their power. In terms of their status, it may be that the title 'care assistant' does not help; low pay is another contributory factor to low status. Training may be improving, but we seem to find difficulty in making staff feel important and valued in the task that they do.

A part of the explanation for this is that they are all so busy. At the risk of generalising, it still is not always seen as part of the job to chat to residents. You've got to be busy, you've got to be dusting, you've got to polishing, you've got be lifting, you've got to be bathing. The result is that people feel guilty about stopping to chat. Quite often when they do stop to talk, they hear something that disturbs them about another staff member who was said to be a bit rough in toileting or bathing. If the staff member is told something like this, the alarm bells ring but as with most of us in the morning, we switch them off quickly. 'No, it couldn't be Mary or John that did that.' 'Well, perhaps Mary or John had a bad day; it was probably a one-off.' The reality is that it may not have been.

In fact there are considerable problems consequent on the term 'complaining'. You would never get away with it in the world of social care but I would love to see the development of an alternative style of expressing concern, something I would call *a moans procedure*! How such an activity could be dignified is uncertain, but it has a place somewhere. Somehow the threat of being complained about has to be managed in a different way - which will not happen while we suspend people without thought to the consequences. Actions taken by agencies often are out of all proportion to what 'the complainants' wanted. Service users tell me that they would never have complained if they had known what the 'town hall' people were going to do. 'All I wanted them to do was to tell him off', they say. But now senior managers are scared. If something does not happen soon, we will return to the most institutional type care imaginable. Staff in residential homes will stop touching residents, which may already have happened in many child care establishments. I can imagine in elderly persons' homes that the effect of the common market directive in respect of manual lifting will be that residents will be put in hoists and sent across the lounge. It will be rather like those devices in shops where you used to put the money in a carton at the counter and it went whizzing across on a wire to a cashier in an office. Staff will be saying 'Fred's on the way'. Wham! Staff will not get into too much trouble provided that they do not leave some poor soul half way across the room.

I view residential care as a good service, a service that is going to be greatly needed. Yet it does need rescuing from its present plight. There are a lot of staff doing a really good job but the few who are not will attract all the publicity. Sometimes as I listen at enquiries to the events that are shown to have happened, I cannot understand how people could be so horrid. Nor do I always understand how they got in the service in the first place. Of course starting to work in a residential home can be very easy; at times it is an absolute doddle to become a care assistant in an old people's home and then have the power that I have described. Many people are not in the least bothered about the calibre of people working in a residential home until suddenly they are considering whether it is appropriate for their mother, their father or themselves to be placed in a residential home. People are thinking more and more about that, including the financing of it, and certainly the government is. What the life-style in a residential home should be like is for debate. What has surprised me is the realisation that some of today's ideas have their roots in the past. For example, I thought the hotel model of residential care was new. But at a conference of the Social Services Policy Forum, Sally Sainsbury traced the roots of legislation for adults. She said that after 1945 when the Labour Party were looking at what they might do in the welfare state, Bevan said that he wanted the poorer class to have what the middle classes had. And one of the things that the middle classes had was a hotel. So we must make hotels available to the poorer classes. There are people who will choose that sort of environment and have the finances for it. Yet a 'hotel model' may imply minimal staff assistance. Indeed, one of the central debates in our society surrounds the expectations that we may have of 'care'. Come what may, residential work will be in business for a long time to come.

The model or style of practice within a home influences daily life: there are consequences for the how people live, work and cope which, in turn, affect the chances of things going wrong. There are a range of models and a range of resident and staff abilities. I am one of the people who, many years back, argued that it was appropriate for people who are elderly mentally infirm to be cared for in ordinary, everyday residential care homes. I have to acknowledge that I was wrong and think that I should have realised this earlier. We are going to have to return to specialisation because lack of specialisation will in itself be another reason why residential care will fester. It is of particular importance that demented elderly people have the same basic care as anyone else. But I do not think there can be much doubt that, given the situation and people's anxiety relating to wandering, some special thought has to be given to their environment. Indeed, I am just about to give evidence in a civil case where an elderly person wandered and fell off the top of the fire escape; she died and the home owner is being sued.

This leads to another area which often is the subject of investigations: restraint. I should like be able to state that restraint is always wrong, and in many cases, perhaps most cases, I will. However, there has to be an outer fabric by which we can ensure safety for everyone. Many homes now have press button types of locks. That in itself is interesting because very recently I found myself locked in a residential home for fifteen minutes! I believe that there are ways and means that are acceptable and dignified that can ensure that we keep people safe. The people who have played the largest part in convincing me are service users. There are some residents amongst those with most of their faculties who report to me specific examples of the problems which occur. For example, they cite one of the problems as people being unable to differentiate between what is acceptable behaviour and what is not, a confusion which has implications for understanding the reasons why abuse occurs.

My position is that the behaviour I am looking for from staff must apply to all residents; there must be the same dignity, privacy and autonomy. The response I get from the residents is, 'Yes, but at 6 o'clock this morning Mary, the care assistant, got a good hiding from another resident. What was she supposed to do? She didn't do anything but she took it out on the rest of us for the rest of the day'. Now that can happen in any setting. People will be moody. People are human. People are different. And I would not want to see any establishment in existence where staff greet me to me on arrival with the phrase, 'We seek to treat everyone the same'. That must be repulsive and there are still places that make that claim. They think that it is going to impress me. My response is that staff will like some people more than others, and that their professionalism will be shown in their ability to operate in a way that residents will feel that they have been treated fairly.

It is essential that the topic of abuse in residential homes is set firmly in the context of the depths to which we can plummet in homes for elderly people. One investigation I have undertaken started from an allegation that someone had been left on the toilet for four hours. Subsequently a further forty five matters of poor practice were found. The events had taken place in a home for physically disabled people. When I questioned what had happened, I was told that the resident had to be challenged to use her independence. She was capable in their view of going to the toilet and so she had to learn the hard way. I did not find that acceptable. The dividing line between independence and neglect can be a very thin one.

Another illustration is of what might be termed poor practice rather than abuse. I was a governor of an establishment for people without sight. On arrival for a meeting one day, I spotted a young lady who was wearing one green fluorescent sock and one pink one, which shows how long ago this was because it was in the days when fluorescent socks were fashionable! When I asked her key worker about it, he replied, 'It's her choice'. I said, 'Does she know she's got a green one on and a pink one?' The dialogue continued as follows:

> 'No'.
> 'Have you told her?'
> 'No, she chose which socks she wanted to put on'.

My reaction was very strong. This is an example of neglect muddled up with independence. Independence must be pursued as far as possible, but there must be limits.

It is so easy in a residential home to be unaware of the implications of actions and words. Making a remark to one person that can be a laugh and a joke, may cause terrible harm and upset to the person in the next room. I am a Scouser and Scousers are known for fairly raucous language and raucous behaviour. I was in an establishment where I had gone to check on the change-over of staff and I arrived at five in the morning, an illustration of the hours people put in on investigations. I was greeted by a care assistant being knocked back against the wall, hit by a service user. I thought that the staff member handled it tremendously well. Not long afterwards the senior care officer came on duty and let rip at the elderly man who had hit the care assistant and, to be fair, the elderly man let rip back at her and they had a good old bit of repartee. While this was going on I walked along the corridor and the lady in the next room was in floods of tears because she thought next door a fight was going on. And it wasn't. When I questioned the senior care officer, she said to me, 'He'll think something's wrong if I don't "F and blind" at him in the morning'. When I asked about consequences elsewhere round the building, she said that she had never thought about it.

Another terrible event at a different home was to watch the procedures for breakfast . The first course had been completed and the slops were put into a plastic bucket. My colleague was watching how the breakfast was continuing to be served and saw that, later, the porridge was served from the same bucket. What possible justification can there be? The justification I was given, incredible as it may sound, was that there were insufficient staff. Many of the people who sit across the table from me and say these sort of things at enquiries have been in the service working in residential homes for ten or fifteen years. Sadly, there are also many people who are described as the salt of the earth who let this sort of thing go on. So we are faced with question, 'How is this to be stopped?'

It is my belief that social care differs little in this respect from other services and that there is as much abuse and poor practice in other public services. There are some key objectives relating to abuse:

- We have to ensure that abuse will be difficult to undertake;
- when abuse has occurred, it must be detected relatively easily;
- to do that, we have to give people confidence that if they complain, they will not be shunned or put aside;
- further, the complainants need to feel that the end of the world has not come if they themselves are complained about;
- service users and relatives need to feel that they have been listened to.

Such procedures must take account of the capacity of the residents as I have seen seemingly excellent complaints procedures in an establishment that did not take account of the fact that the majority of service users could not speak or write. There was no advocacy system to go with it.

The doors of residential homes must be opened without breaking people's privacy. For this to happen there must be an appreciation of the difference between different parts of the home: thus, there is a distinction between the lounge of a residential home for elderly people which is a public place and the bedrooms and the private areas which are not. People must be helped to feel more confident about what is going on behind those doors so that, for example, relatives can know what is going on and not feel guilty that their mother or father is living in residential care. Typically, establishments are not good either at allowing people to see what is happening or at having comments about what is known. On numerous occasions and put in all sorts of ways I have heard people told: 'If you don't like what we're doing, perhaps you'd like to take her home'. What is said may not be put quite as starkly as that, but that is what it means.

We are going to have to ensure that people who care for others in the way that I have described, undertaking the most private tasks, have an element of training that is a more than 'What to do when the fire bell goes off'. Training of staff continues to be a difficulty. There is a need for basic training, for example in fire precaution and action, but this must include consideration of the wider systems so that people who are saved from being burnt, do not break their arms getting through the fire door. It is necessary to recognise that even with regard to basic training such as training in toileting or lifting, only small proportions of staff have been trained. The Social Care Association produced some figures which showed that under ten per cent of care staff had had such training. There are understandable but nevertheless unacceptable reasons for this: everyone is so busy, staff cannot be got together because of shifts or night staff. It remains essential that staff are trained and appreciate the significance of the way that they work. Of course, staff motivation plays a part: some people will see the work as 'just a job' and in my experience that is more the case in London. For many others it is not. They see it as important to get the pay packet at the end of the week or the end of the month, but they do have a far greater involvement than that. The message must be given out to let people know how important they are and what status and power they have got in dealing with other people's lives.

At this stage I want to move to consider organisational influences. An aspect that is distinctive to local authorities is the visit of the elected representative, the local councillor. Visits by councillors may play a part in uncovering things that are wrong but by their nature they have severe limitations. Members need advice as to what to look for because otherwise the focus of such visits is on the concrete: 'Look we haven't had this done for X Y and Z'. A better system for organising such visits would be for visits to be carried out by the ward councillors. The people living in the home are a part of the councillor's electorate. Certainly it would be helpful for elected members to be trained to examine whether some significant factors are not being glossed over. The same has to be done by line managers, assistant directors, directors of social services, and heads of organisations.

The critical issue is not the type of organisation in which people work about which a lot of hot air has been expended. If people are in the work for profit they get one type of money, if they are in local government, they get a wage. It does not matter where the work is done, as long as that work is done properly. It is possible in the independent sector to cut out some of the bureaucracy. In terms of training I suggest that the independent sector is being treated unfairly at the moment in terms of money available to it. The training support grant, provided through the Department of Health and currently available only to local government, should be made equally available to the independent sector. The independent sector cannot be expected to be able to train its staff in financial terms in the same way as local government. Residential care will remain in the public eye if for no other reason than that of people having to sell their houses to finance it. There is an opportunity to try to restore confidence in its organisation and practice. There are many ways to do this, such as the proposal for a general social services council; however it is done the task is vital for the protection of the public and to monitor the quality of residential care.

I conclude by focusing back on the task of carrying out investigations. Many of them have taken over a year. The consequences for staff afterwards are enormous. You cannot in my view afford to take that sort of time. Investigations have to be carried out thoroughly, competently and quickly and into the process should be built procedures so that staff that have been subject to allegation and are cleared are helped, and so that action is taken quickly against those who are not cleared. It is the job of myself and others like me to try to ensure that poor staff and malicious staff do not work in residential care. But at the end of the day the prime responsibility of course is with those who work with them, and those who employ them.

Acknowledgement

This chapter is based on the text of a speech given at the Lancaster Conference. I am grateful to Roger Clough for work on editing the material.

Thirteen

Managing enquiries

John Osborne

AN EVENT AND ITS REPERCUSSIONS

Some years ago as a line manager for a number of residential homes for older people, I was called upon to deal with a particularly serious and complex incident of abuse. Working with the Officer in Charge, it soon became apparent that a full scale enquiry was needed. Further, we thought it important to engage a consultant who could assist with the complex organisational perspectives that were in play. What followed was the work mentioned above by Elisabeth Henderson (Chapter 8). The enquiry, the consultation, and the work that developed proved the beginning of a long hard struggle first to get people to listen and accept that abuse had taken place and, secondly, to take the appropriate action. Despite many stumbling blocks the fact that the Lancaster conference took place at all is a tribute to the staying power, commitment and dogged determination of those determined to raise the profile of this issue.

The writing of this short paper has reminded me of the struggles in undertaking investigations and the problems and obstacles that can be placed in the way. It takes the form of an attempt to highlight some of the key points and to list some potentially 'helpful hints' for those who become involved in similar work in the future.

THE INCIDENT

The event that triggered the enquiry was of a sexual nature involving two residents, a man and a woman who had severe dementia. Immediately it became apparent that this was not an isolated incident. What was uncovered was a history of continuous systematic abuse by this particular male resident over a ten year period. Consistently this man had chosen victims who were female residents with dementia and thus unable to speak out for themselves.

It was a complex situation which finally necessitated a formal enquiry. From this it became clear that other professionals had previously identified elements of abusive behaviour. Some had been unable to report this effectively because they did not accept that this level of sexual activity could take place amongst older people. Others did not have the language to report what happened; they preferred to use vague euphemisms either through embarrassment or lack of formal knowledge. A further group genuinely appeared to have failed to understand; that is they misread the signals of what was going on around them, or preferred to adopt the 'group' position rather than acknowledge their individual awareness. Elisabeth Henderson emphasises this point in her paper.

In understanding this incident and the work that followed it is essential to consider the whole subject of sexual abuse and older people.

SEXUAL ABUSE

Increasingly it is becoming accepted that some older people are the victims of abuse, and that this abuse can take a variety of forms: staff of resident, resident of staff and of one resident by another resident. Yet we hear little of the sexual abuse of older people. Frank Glendenning (Chapter 4) emphasises the importance of recognising the existence of the sexual abuse of older people. In doing this we must:

- look at issues of sexuality in old age: these are affected by our own ageism and the taboo that remains around this subject;
- examine and accept our individual responses and the personal baggage that we bring to the situation;
- recognise the need for staff training that is relevant and provides an element of healing;
- realise that we cannot 'paper over the cracks': we need to

acknowledge the damage that may have been done to staff in the course of their work and expect to deal with this either before, or within, the context of specific training.

THE WAY FORWARD

Perhaps one of the principal challenges in residential care and nursing homes is to consider ways in which we can develop systems that are more open and less blaming. We must consider how we can encourage people to break the silence. The aim is not to punish or scapegoat but to reinforce the primary task: that is to act in the interests of the older people who live in the homes.

SETTING UP AN INVESTIGATION

On starting an investigation it is useful to develop a 'working brief' in consultation with one's line manager. This should include the remit for the work that is to be undertaken, the reporting framework and the resource implications. It may be necessary for the investigator to step out of their usual duties temporarily whilst the investigation takes place. If an agreement (and possibly resources) are secured from the line manager, the task becomes one for the organisation and not one for an individual to juggle personally.

As some investigations may yield difficult and disturbing facts about the current or past running of the organisation, it is essential that ownership of the investigation rests within the organisation. Thus, the individual is protected from being seen as the one who is 'the problem'. Whilst it may be extremely difficult for someone who believes abuse to have occurred to call a halt to an investigation that has started, it is imperative that the consequences of working outside an agreed remit are not ignored: these may be marginalisation and an undermining of the investigation. In these circumstances stopping the abuse becomes almost impossible. If the enquiry is conducted within the hierarchical structure of the organisation and managers agree the steps to be taken, it becomes much more difficult to 'close down' an investigation. In addition, the individual will have covered her/himself from possible allegations of personal interference or over-zealousness

Within the working brief it is useful to consider the need for external consultation for oneself and other members of the investigating team. Often the details of abuse cases are distressing, and they can set off painful memories for residents, staff and investigators. Much of this pain may be left with the person undertaking the investigation. A safe place to examine and contain these feelings is essential if they are not to cloud the investigation and adversely affect one's ability to deal clearly and effectively with the job in hand.

CARRYING OUT AN INVESTIGATION

It is easy to assume that people will find out the facts from each other. The reality is that the investigator must ensure that everyone has the same information, unless there are sound reasons why certain, probably confidential, information is not passed to everyone. It may be helpful to construct a paragraph outlining the purpose of your investigation and, where possible, the incident that started it. Ensuring that everyone has heard the facts as they are known to the investigator will help to avoid confusion, rumour and misinformation.

When undertaking an investigation, language must be specific, jargon avoided and plain language used that is easily understood. The person conducting the enquiry must check that each individual understands the meaning of what is being said even when the detail is sexually explicit and may be perceived as awkward or embarrassing. It must not be assumed that everyone will understand all that is being said. Given the sensitive nature of the subject, often staff feel more comfortable speaking in euphemisms such as, 'She's got a bit of a problem down below', than in direct or specific language. By playing down the language used because it is more comfortable or less embarrassing, the information being communicated can also be down played, with potentially serious consequences.

CONCLUDING AN INVESTIGATION

When setting up an investigation it is important to bear in mind what is to happen to the information that is uncovered, and to record and document evidence with this in mind. There is no use coming to the end of an exhaustive investigation and realising that the records are inadequate in that they have not captured some of the most important evidence in a way that is of use once the investigation stage is complete. Again the use of a working brief is a useful way of addressing this issue at the outset.

It is important to consider to whom the report is to be made: is this to be the line manager or the Director? Consideration should also be given to methods of communicating findings to peers and colleagues involved in residential work with other client groups.

The probability is that for staff an investigation will be difficult and demanding: what feed-back do they need to be given and in what form? Similarly, the other residents, their families and carers will know that something is going on; indeed, they may have been directly involved. They too need to be told formally of the outcome of an investigation and to be reassured by the action that is to be taken to avoid such an occurrence in the future.

In concluding the investigation, an action plan needs to be produced outlining the work that needs to be undertaken in order of priority:

- who should be responsible for particular actions?
- are there time constraints or targets?
- how is wider ownership of the problem to be promoted?
- what are the ways to seek to enlist senior manager commitment to moving forward on action identified?

All too often excellent investigations are fed into organisations which fail to act on the findings and seem to see the act of conducting the investigation as a way of preventing repetition of events in the future. Placed alongside the detail of an investigation, an action plan will have a much greater impact and may stand a greater chance of implementation. Included in the action plan should be an outline of resource implications. It may be useful to summarise what are thought to be the consequences of *failing* to take any action.

What I have tried to do is use my experience (with the dilemmas I have faced) to examine the components and characteristics of what is an extremely difficult and stressful task. I have had in mind the needs of those who are courageous and committed enough to ensure that abuse is identified and dealt with whenever it occurs and my determination that such people should have the maximum support available. Of course there are other many other features that will assist a successful investigation. I have not tried to write a comprehensive manual but to set out factors that I regard as essentials.

Fourteen

Bad apple or sick building? Management responses to institutional abuse

Lorayne Ferguson

In this chapter I consider two different ways of understanding and analysing abuse that happens in residential establishments. These are in effect two diagnostic models of institutional abuse, which I term the bad apple and the sick building. Working from this, I consider alternative styles of management response and the implications for residents' empowerment.

The home which I use as a case study below, is based on a real place and real events; however names and some details are changed to ensure anonymity.

THE INSTITUTION

This adult home, which for our purposes shall rejoice in the name Falklands House, is old and dilapidated. It has an ageing hot water and heating system which functions erratically. Many rooms have been without hot water for months.

Falklands House was built in the days when residential care was intended for elderly people who were mainly self-caring. Today few residents are self-caring and many are suffering from physical and/or mental impairment. They require considerable personal care and supervision but the home has seen few changes, or staff increases, to reflect this. Its future is now uncertain. The Social Services Department (for it is indeed a local authority home) may decide to refurbish and upgrade but it is equally likely to close it: too old, too large, too smelly to be worth saving.

Then a decision is made. The home will close in eighteen months. No new residents are admitted, no new staff are recruited. Agency staff fill the gaps.

THE STAFF

The Officer in Charge, what with long service annual leave entitlement, study leave and sickness, has not been much in evidence. The day-to-day running has been delegated to the senior officers who are under a great deal of pressure coping with staff conflicts, staff shortages, new demands in terms of health and safety, manual handling, and COSHH regulations and budget monitoring, as well as the administration of large quantities of medication. For those senior staff who have been in post for many years, the job barely resembles the one they originally undertook. The new, young, senior officer has little in common with her colleagues or their style.

Staff are not involved in decision making. Morale is low.

THE DIAGNOSIS

All of the above may sound familiar to those having even a casual acquaintance with local authority care of elderly people. But what you may not have noticed is that Falklands House conforms exactly to Roger Clough's profile of indicators common to those establishments subject to serious abuse enquiries (Clough; 1988):

- the establishment is run down, appears uncared for (a pervasive smell of urine)
- there are staff shortages and staff sickness
- senior staff are on holiday
- there is little supervision of staff
- staff have been in charge of the unit with considerable autonomy for a long time
- there is uncertainty about the future of the establishment
- there have been changes in the task of the centre
- there is discord among the staff team.

And there is more. Another of Clough's indicators is that 'there has been a series of complaints, particularly if they relate to different aspects of daily living and relate to more than one member of staff'. This was indeed the case at Falklands House. Inspectors, senior managers, families, and the multidisciplinary team all complained about the poor quality of care. There was an extraordinary number of accidents to residents.

And still there is more. Wardaugh and Wilding (1993) identified these indicators for a 'corruption of care':

1. *The corruption of care depends upon the neutralisation of normal moral concerns*
   Those responsible for Falklands House found it acceptable to house elderly people in shoddy smelly surroundings. Many members of staff viewed residents as 'demanding'. As so often happens, they blamed the victim, thereby legitimising the deterioration in care.
2. *The corruption of care is closely connected with the balance of power and powerlessness in organisations*
   Staff at Falklands House felt powerless. They had given up fighting – even for a proper hot water supply. Because their own status as fully moral beings was undermined by powerlessness, they ceased to behave in a fully moral fashion.
3. *Management failure underlies the corruption of care*
   As we are about to see, management's failure was almost complete.

SENIOR MANAGEMENT'S RESPONSE

What is extraordinary about management's response to these diagnostic indicators (and why I have gone into such detail about them) is that they missed them entirely. Either that or they were simply too afraid to utter the word 'abuse'. Whichever, they outwardly defined the problem solely in terms of poor management – our old friend The Bad Apple.

Their first action was to send the Officer in Charge on yet another training course. Some in-house sessions were provided for care staff. Action plans were drawn up, and supervision was to be stepped up. But nothing changed; in fact staff absence through sickness actually increased. After yet another complaint, the Officer in Charge was suspended and an independent inquiry set up.

The inquiry certainly did catalogue serious management failures, but it also uncovered widespread abuse. Residents' basic needs for personal care, respect, independence and consideration were frequently ignored. Mealtimes were a noisy shambles. Cold water washes were common. Records showed serious neglect of a very ill resident. And then there were all those accidents.

But still management was thinking in terms of 'bad apples', that is that the problem lay with individuals who contaminated others, not with systems or cultures. In fact it seems likely that a prime motivating force behind the independent inquiry was to gather evidence for disciplinary charges. While this was going on a series of temporary managers ran Falklands House, each staying only a few months. After six months the officer in charge left.

What I am suggesting is that senior management got it wrong twice, or at least one mistake led to another. They thought the problem was poor management (not abuse) so they sought out the bad apple, not the culture.

During the Lancaster Conference considerable emphasis was placed on the role of the culture of an establishment in permitting abuse to take place in the first instance, and then allowing its perpetuation. In one workshop the rotten apple metaphor was extended to look at how the apple contaminated others it touched. Contamination could be said only to happen if the climate was conducive – warm and moist. If the barrel was being maintained under proper conditions – cool and crisp – the rot could not spread. At the risk of stretching the metaphor beyond its limits, one might examine the other individual apples for surface bruising which could indicate a propensity for contamination. The important message, however, is the relevance of the culture – or climate – to the perpetuation and spread of abuse, rather than the presence of the rotten apple. This is what I call 'the sick building model of institutional abuse'.

AN ALTERNATIVE STRATEGY

What is noteworthy about what happened next at Falklands House is that it happened by accident – like the discovery of penicillin. I want to argue that it could, up to a point, be replicated.

What happened was this. Another new manager arrived, but this time she wasn't alone. She brought with her a group of staff and residents from the home which she has managed for several years. That home was being refurbished and it was convenient to 'decant' some staff and residents while the work was done. Falklands House, half empty because of its proposed closure, was the obvious receptacle for this decanting. The new arrivals made up approximately one third of both staff and residents. The staff encompassed the full range: officer in charge, senior staff, night staff, daycare and domestics.

In three months improvements occurred which no previous manager had achieved. The physical environment, the systems, some of this had been addressed, but the culture was only now beginning to change. The sick building was on the mend, and perhaps not coincidentally the new regime began with the look of the place. New paint and wallpaper announced to all: 'We may soon close; but residents, staff and families deserve better than this – they are of value'.

The crucial factor, though, in turning the tide was that those 'old' Falklands House staff who had struggled all along to maintain good care practices now have real support at all levels. They are no longer outweighed by others who do not share their approach. There have been positive alliances formed with the incoming staff who have come from a home where standards are high and the culture positive.

Those Falklands staff prepared to perpetuate poor practices are now being challenged both by newcomers and from within their own former staff group. New standards are being set by the peer groups of care and domestic staff. The new manager and those senior staff she brought with her are much more in evidence (than were the original senior team) and they are positively reinforcing the improvements. Her style is consultative and staff are actively involved in the allocation of work and in the conduct of day-to-day care.

But perhaps the most exciting and heartening factor is that the culture change is being vigorously promoted by the new cohort of relocated residents. These 'imported' residents are accustomed to being listened to, to being consulted, and to exercising some real control. These residents can be heard saying: 'I want to chose my own clothes'; 'You shouldn't talk like that to me'; 'I will go when I am ready'. Falklands' staff are being confronted with a new kind of resident, and learning how to respond.

So, do we have to accept that this happy accident was a 'one off' and cannot be replicated? I think it is too important a lesson for that, and ways must be found to replicate it at least in part. Common sense ought to tell us that no Wonderwoman or Superman can, on their own, cure a 'sick building'. But from where will our rescue teams come?

My suggestion is that any authority with a number of establishments may well consider identifying, from within its own resources, a group of staff recognised as having the potential for this team role. The process of recognition in this way will enhance their self worth, serving to equip them further for the task ahead. The mechanisms for staff secondment and exchange are there, and have been used from time to time, but only in an ad hoc fashion. I am proposing a more formal arrangement whereby a number of secondments would be made in order to transform an abusive culture by an intervention of the kind received by Falklands House.

Depending on the circumstances the team would need to include an officer in charge supported by at least one person at team leader level. The numbers and deployment of care staff, night staff and domestics will be determined by the extent and location of the problem culture. In most circumstances a team of between six and ten secondees should have the necessary impact.

It would obviously be preferable for the team already to know one another, but unless the circumstances were identical to my case study, it is unlikely a team could be drawn from one establishment. However, professionalism, trust, and personal strength will carry people a long way, especially where the task in hand offers such rewards. It is also important that the intervention lasts for at least a year, which will prevent the old guard from simply waiting for them to leave. As a consequence, new alliances will be formed. The team members will need to be covered by agency staff or locums on short term contracts. Part of the cost of this can be recouped by a vacancy discount in the target home, but even so there will be a price.

Which brings us back to why I called this home Falklands House. If we think something is important enough – something in the national interest – we can will the means.

It will be more difficult to replicate the role of the residents even though I believe this to be of equal importance. Clearly it would be both impracticable and insupportable to contrive a situation where any group of residents should be moved from one home in order to help challenge deficiencies in a culture in another – they cannot be considered part of the team, though it is possible that some might wish to play a part. Yet we should not ignore the potential value of holiday exchanges as a way of enhancing the openness of a more closed and insular establishment. Those residents who are staying on a holiday have little to fear from doing a bit of stirring or moaning about practices which may prevail in their temporary home. And their expectations that they had a right to be heard may help change a climate in which staff had grown accustomed to forgetting that residents are individuals with rights and preferences.

Managers should think boldly where exchanges are concerned. They could 'twin' with homes in other parts of the UK or in Europe. I have recently had experience of a group of residents from Belgium staying in a home in England. They were astonished to find that wine and beer were not offered with every meal!

One of Wardaugh and Wilding's indicators alerted us to the danger of an enclosed, inward-looking organisation. Clough identified few visitors, few contacts and few visits out as warning signs. What we can learn from this is that authorities should make more of a real commitment to exchanges and holiday opportunities.

Finally, there are things we can be doing to empower our residents—not just because it is a good thing in itself but because it is their first line of defence against abuse.

At Lancaster, workshop members identified some of the ways in which this can be encouraged, and there will be examples of good practice scattered across the country. For example, the involvement of residents' committees and residents' meetings in (meaningful) ways. Not the kind of residents' meetings held at Falklands House where the minutes showed that month after month simple requests for curtains in the dining room and for a menu to be displayed went totally unheeded.

There are other mechanisms: the use of advocates; the development of formal, internal quality monitoring systems; the provision of pre-admission information which emphasises residents' rights endorsed by active promotion and monitoring following admission; reviews which are more than just window-dressing or rubber-stamping; the involvement of residents' visitors and families; and proper complaints systems.

Dick Clough's suggestion for a 'moans procedure' (p146) is attractive. It seems to allow residents to participate in an activity which could bring about change without necessarily invoking the full might of the disciplinary procedures. It also conforms more to the sick building model than to the bad apple model. Residents themselves have said that they did not want to get individual members of staff into trouble, they just wanted the problem solved. Residents are closer to staff than senior management could ever be, and because they witness the day-to-day pressures on staff, their sympathies are often with them too. They may well have understood for some time that problems occur when systems fail and permit abuse to remain unchallenged. It is no doubt easier for them to speak up against an abusive culture (however they define it) than against named individuals, and what I am proposing is that they should be encouraged to do so.

None of these measures alone can be expected to achieve the aim of enabling elderly residents and their families always to feel able to contribute, or to challenge staff or establishment practices. But the wider the range of measures made available, the more likely it is that each individual will find a way to participate, to find his or her voice and, should the need arise, to say: 'You cannot do this to me'.

Fifteen

Training residential staff to be aware of sexual abuse in old age

Hazel J Ker

INTRODUCTION

This paper is not intended to be a complete outline of a potential training programme but to raise issues for consideration when designing a programme to promote understanding of sexual abuse in old age. Currently there exists little or no material.

Training on all abuse issues in old age must be undertaken within the context of the way in which our society defines old age, our own attitudes to ageing and, indeed, our own ageism.

CONTEXT

In considering sexuality in old age we are faced with a 'double whammy' taboo: first, there is denial and non-acceptance of older people's value and continuing involvement in life; in addition, sexuality in old age is even less accepted and acknowledged. What images exist around us which present sexual relationships as a normal part of the ageing process? In particular there is little information available on the problems faced by individuals who are deprived of their long term sexual partner due to illness or death. A notable exception is Age Concern's *Living, Loving and Ageing* with accompanying video. An essential preliminary to any study of abuse is an exploration of what is considered normal and acceptable, including awareness of the needs of homosexual relationships. Discussion of sexuality should lead to our facing up to individual responses. These will vary for each participant. It is important to be aware of the varying cultural and religious expectations of staff, service users and their carers and families.

STRUCTURE AND SETTING: THE NOTION OF HEALING

When staff have been witness to sexual abuse in a professional or a personal sense, effective training needs to contain within it an element of healing. This can be developed in several ways:

Preparation
The content of the training is likely to engender strong personal responses such as distress, denial ('I don't believe people behave like that'; 'I've never seen him/her do that') or even non-participation. Engaging with participants prior to the training event on a one-to-one basis, gives them an opportunity to raise concerns and prepare themselves for the training;

Setting clear boundaries and ground rules at the start for all participants
The terms and conditions of participation must be made explicit, including the potential consequences of disclosure of personal information.

Careful pacing of training
Ensuring individuals can participate when they feel comfortable to do so - this would be enhanced by a modular approach:

- The provision of both a safe place and a safe person to talk through personal and sometimes painful experiences: for example, one training programme included the presence of a trained counsellor from the welfare section of the organisation; ideally, the counsellor should be available throughout the training course;
- Recognition that learning continues beyond the formal training event: access to further support may be necessary, for example:

    1. at the work place through supervision;
    2. ongoing access to a trainer or counsellor; *or*
    3. appropriate referral to other agencies;

- Enabling participants to reflect on how they might communicate sensitively on this subject with service users: there may be differences between resident and staff member not only of age but also of gender, race, culture and religious belief.

GROWING OLD

A proper understanding of the process of ageing, including the effects of dementia and mental illness, is crucial to an understanding of sexual behaviour in old age. Sexual abuse occurs for different reasons. On the one hand, the person who perpetrates abuse may have been an abuser all his life or, on the other hand, the abusive behaviour may be the result of disinhibition factors linked to dementia or mental illness. It is essential to be able to recognise and understand the differences: life long abusers do not stop simply because they get old. Two points are important. The first is that I use the word 'he' to recognise that the overwhelming majority of people who sexually abuse others are men. Secondly an understanding of abuse does not imply toleration.

Dementia is no respecter of class, cultural or religious norms: relatives can be extremely distressed when confronted with the non-repressed sexual behaviour or language of a parent. Similarly, such understanding is also important for the needs of potential victims, in particular because they may no longer be able to speak for themselves. How might they complain? What are the indicators of distress for different individuals? How protected are they in their living situation?

The participants on a course also need to consider how older people can be encouraged to speak out about personal concerns such as inappropriate sexual behaviour, bearing in mind their upbringing and socialisation.

LANGUAGE

Besides the obvious need to avoid jargon it is essential to ensure that participants:

1. Do understand what is being said; *and*
2. Feel comfortable enough to ask questions and express themselves in familiar language.

The English language abounds with euphemisms for sexual

acts and intimate parts of the human body . Terms vary by generation: words chosen by a ninety year old woman to describe sexual intercourse are likely to be very different to those used by her teenage grandson; they also vary by region, culture and religion. Such variations in language may be localised even down to families, which may invent their own 'acceptable' language. Different cultures and religions may have clearly defined limits of what is acceptable and what is not in both words and actions. Whilst all this serves to underline the taboo nature of the subject within our society, it also means that clear and effective communication is made difficult.

This lack of commonality in language leads to misunderstandings and misperception which are particularly important in considering the reporting of incidents of abuse, both verbally and in writing. Indeed, such lack of clarity appears to be at odds with the images of our society as sexually explicit and open. For example, although the words 'bugger' and 'buggery' were frequently bandied about in personal banter between care staff, it became clear on a training programme that some of them did not understand the specific meanings of the terms. Nor was there always clarity as to the appropriate technical words for male and female genitalia.

In order to be able to report an incident precisely to other members of staff and co-professionals such as medical personnel, psycho-geriatricians and the police, or, indeed, even to be able to raise concerns about what is or is not appropriate sexual behaviour, staff must be practised in using the appropriate language effectively and without being self-conscious. In talking to service users and their families in a way that makes them feel comfortable, different words may have to be used to create an appropriate language.

THE RESIDENTIAL SETTING

It is important to recognise that the structure and function of the institution itself (be it residential or nursing home) can provide opportunities for abuse. Someone who has been what I have termed a life time abuser will be practised and skilled in abusing others. It is possible that abusers of this type may be less likely than other people to have developed extended support networks and therefore may be more likely to live in a residential home. Being aware of a resident's previous life history may aid recognition of potential abusers.

The residential setting provides the abuser with a number of potential victims who are residents because of their vulnerability and need for protection. An abuser will know the pattern of the day when staff are least likely to be around: hand-overs; answering a call bell at the other end of the building; night time when less staff are on duty. Staff need to be aware of the potential of such situations and consider how to provide maximum care and protection.

IDENTIFICATION AND INTERVENTION

The main objective of the training programme will be to enable staff to identify abusive sexual behaviour and to intervene effectively and sensitively either to prevent its occurrence or to respond quickly after the event.

This means recognising that sexual behaviour in itself is not inappropriate; it becomes inappropriate and abusive when it is not sought, or when it is experienced as inappropriate or even offensive. If residents are not able to express their views then the role of staff or others as arbiters is even more crucial. There are occasions when staff may allow male residents to continue with unwanted sexual approaches, because they assume different things about older people than they do about other adults. For example, they may be unwilling to confront the men 'because they are old' or they may think that older women who are confused 'don't really know what is going on'.

Whatever activities such as case studies or role plays are set up to examine abuse, meaningful exploration can only take place when the context, structure, and language of the training programme have been given full consideration.

As well as recognising what constitutes abusive behaviour, staff will need to know the actions to take when this behaviour becomes an offence: for example, when are other agencies such as police or doctors to be involved? Some agencies do have guidelines which help to clarify this, but many do not.

If staff themselves in their training have felt that their individual responses have been encouraged and dealt with sensitively and with understanding , they in turn are more likely to respond to residents and relatives with sensitivity and understanding. Thus, staff will need to understand that the range of responses from families and relatives can be as varied as their own: denial, not wanting to know or anger. The families of the abusers may be hostile to staff or blame them for failure to protect the victim. This can be compounded by an anxiety or fear of 'losing the bed' and not wanting to create waves or cause trouble, particularly if outside agencies become involved.

In working in an area that is so little acknowledged, staff will need to recognise they are likely to be the 'experts'. As such they may need to become skilled advocates on behalf of service users and their families and learn how to develop effective support networks for all concerned.

POLICIES AND PROCEDURES

Training should result in staff becoming confident as to how to act in the future. This means that any training programme must be linked to organisational policies and procedures and recognise the necessity of these. Also, managers within the organisation need to be aware of and understand the potential for sexual abuse in old age, so that they can communicate effectively with, and most importantly respond to, care staff and service users.

Where policies and procedures are limited or even non existent in relation to sexual abuse, staff and managers need to consider localised and in-unit procedures. These procedures in turn must link to policies that do exist, such as the systems for reporting incidents. In all of this staff need guidance to develop their own practice guidelines:

- Who takes responsibility for what?
- When does an incident need to be reported?
- Does this vary at night time, evenings or weekends?
- Who does the recording and where is this record kept?

The above information is by no means exhaustive but hopefully gives an indication of how to approach a training programme on a subject where there is little information, research or even acknowledgement of its existence.

Sixteen

Issues for further reflection

Olive Stevenson

HOW WIDE, HOW NARROW?

The chapters in this book may well leave the reader, as they do me, wondering as to the most useful focus for our deliberations. On the one hand, people rightly point out that the issue of abuse is part of a much wider problem concerning the position of old people in society, and about good practice in community care. We see how denigration and the low status of elderly people in society and how a social environment which denies them full humanity play their part in creating a climate in which poor or abusive residential care can take root. We have noted particularly, through watching and discussing videos at the Lancaster conference, what a critical part the media plays in this, specifically in reinforcing 'pitiful', 'eccentric' and 'deviant' images of old people and their consequent effect on ageist attitudes. We need no persuading that tackling ageism in society generally and in the professional 'helpers' is crucial. One of my tasks in teaching social work students is quite simply to insist that old people continue to have the powerful feelings, emotional problems which are part of common humanity. Such an obvious point is critical in good residential practice, yet there remains the suggestion that somehow there is a cut off point with retirement and the pension. There is not!

Another virtue of the 'wider' approach is that it enables us to look into the role and context of residential care and ways of creating a climate in it in which old people are valued. Dick Clough asks the important questions: 'How much does the local authority value the residential care which it runs or sponsors?

How much do managers really believe that it can be a good experience for elderly people?' Attitudes of managers can have a very profound effect on the morale of those who work in the institutions. And there can hardly be any doubt that a residential environment where morale is high, and good practice encouraged, is much less likely to be abusive. So I hope everyone will recognise that when we drop a pebble of thought - abuse - into the pond, the ripples spread widely into considerations of practice, policy and attitudes generally.

Yet, (and this is on the other hand), it is clear that there does need to be separate discussion of abuse as such. It is necessary to raise visibility and encourage recognition. It is not simply about a continuum of good to bad practice: somewhere along the line, there is something we will not and cannot tolerate. That is the importance ofGeorge Mabon's assertion that consideration of abuse should be incorporated into procedures about policies, into purchasing and commissioning arrangements and into professional and trade organisations (Chapter Ten).

Separate discussion of abuse is also necessary to pin down more precisely what we are talking about so that we can evolve appropriate strategies to combat it. Should we concentrate mainly on physical and emotional, rather than financial, abuse? There are four different 'scenarios'; abuse by staff on resident; abuse by resident on staff; abuse by resident on resident and, finally, the wider effect of some authorities perhaps abusive policies on staff behaviour to residents, which some believe very important. Such abusive policies may be shown, for example, by depressed staffing levels. Each of these four elements raise very different and very complex questions and we do not serve our cause well if we are imprecise in our analysis.

Thus, in typical academic fashion, I am arguing that we need both the wider and the more focused approach if we are to make progression on this vital subject, bearing in mind that there is a great deal we do not yet know about the context and dynamics of abuse in residential care.

It is for this reason that Anne Craft's paper is important as it brings us up to date with the progress made in the related field of abuse of people with learning disability (Chapter Six). Whilst it will be necessary to study separately issues concerning these groups, it is nonetheless self evident that we have much to learn from each other.

THE IMPLICATIONS FOR MANAGEMENT WITHIN THE RESIDENTIAL CONTEXT

When we consider the 'intolerable', do we seek to distinguish, as George Mabon does, between *abuse* and *harm* in terms of intentionality? I am not sure how helpful that is in terms of action, because understanding the complicated feelings which may give rise to abuse does not alter the fact that some behaviour is unacceptable and must be stopped, whether it be by a harassed member of staff or a person with dementia. It is in what you do afterwards that the intention and state of mind of the staff member become all important. Do you sack them at once? Do you say, 'Well it was a rotten day she was having, her husband had just left her?' One may say - 'If we understand, we cannot blame and therefore we can't do anything'.

This is not true and it is dangerous. Or one may say - 'The action is all important, understanding why is not, so we can discipline people without regard to their situation and feelings.' This is also wrong and dangerous, not least because it leads to a culture of blame, all too apparent at present in some social service organisations. Dick Clough writes of local authorities having gone 'suspension mad', a problem which some of us will readily recognise, especially in cases known to us when the suspended person is subsequently reinstated, after months, with no stain on their character (Chapter 12).

This is a problem which has become apparent across social services departments (but perhaps also in health authorities), an unfortunate side effect of an insistence on greater consumer/ patient rights, which in general we all applaud.

So there is a distinction to be made between prompt and decisive action to stop abuse recurring and considered and sensitive action to deal with its aftermath and impact on all concerned, including the abuser. In line with so much else at the present time, preoccupation with accountability can lead to heavy handed and inappropriate behaviour by managers.

So much of this is, of course, bound up with concept of power. Power is a dominant theme in these papers. Many years ago I wrote an article based on my experience as a young residential worker in a children's home (Stevenson 1972). It seemed to me then that power was always perceived to be somewhere else. Even Kings and Emperors (or Mafia leaders) surround themselves with body guards; as their power increases so does their sense of vulnerability. As one progresses up the hierarchy in health and social service organisations, a sense of powerlessness is still present.

This is particularly true of residential institutions. Think about a prison, in which official power is only maintained by the collusion of the 'residents'. If the residents decide that they are not going to conform, all hell breaks loose. Now it is immediately apparent that in an old people's home, the power of the residents is, in contrast to prison, extremely limited. Nevertheless, it is worth thinking about the power structure in old people's homes when addressing issues of abuse. For example, I have heard a telling example of an old lady who reigned supreme in the sitting room by saying who could go to the toilet and when. If Annie wanted to go the toilet, she would say: 'Sit down, Annie, you've only just been.' And Annie would sit down and then inevitably sooner or later would wet herself. So there was naked power. But there is also the more subtle kind - emotional blackmail, for example, a tool used by some staff to achieve compliance:

It is also worth examining the power structures within the group of care staff. One may get some surprises when one looks at the differences between the official model of management and authority and the other much more complex interactions which affect daily living.

What are we going to do about the feelings of powerlessness of those outside 'in the town hall' who stand outside the home yet have responsibility for it? I have already insisted that there will on occasion be a need for prompt and decisive action to remove an abuser. But for every one of those, there will be many others where a more sensitive and cautions intervention will be called for. If a climate has been created in which, to use Dick Clough's phrase, there may be a perceived difference between 'a moan's procedure' and a 'complaints procedure', it may be possible to address difficulties involving abuse in a more constructive way (p.146). In this context, there has been insufficient discussion of the issue of advocacy. Advocates have a potentially crucial role both in 'moans' and 'complaints' procedures and in distinguishing between the two.

Standing between 'the town hall' and the staff and residents is, of course, the officer in charge or manager, however styled. I do not think the significance of this role has been recognised sufficiently. It is possible to envisage a model in which a home ran so well that the leader would less and less be leading from the front. In this model, the staff and residents become more and more self directed. I love the idea but it seems to me that most of us at present would sleep more happily in our beds if we knew that the leader was exerting a positive and dynamic control over the situation, bearing in mind the rapid turnover of staff in some homes, which makes it difficult to build a stable culture, and the lack of education and training of many care staff. So, if I had limited resources for education and training, I would be inclined to invest them at the level of the manager because lower levels of staff cannot utilise training without support and understanding.

A final point on 'management'; we must recognise that so many of our residents are mentally impaired. Clearly this poses major problems in relation to abuse. One aspect of this is the long haul between total lucidity and total confusion in cases of dementia. This faces care staff and relatives with constant dilemmas concerning the balance between autonomy and protection; talking about `choice', for example, is fine but for some of our residents protection in daily living is more important. And their vulnerability to abuse is frightening.

LEGAL REFORM

In relation to these dilemmas between autonomy and protection, I think that legal reform is imperative. There is a draft Bill to reform the Civil Law, which in my view is more important at present than the Criminal Law, since it is focused on the protection of adults who are no longer competent. The Law Commission (1995) has blazed a trail. It is for all of us now, perhaps using Action on Elder Abuse, to mobilise ourselves to urge that this legislation be enacted.

ORGANISATIONAL DEFENCES AND PERSONAL PAIN

Roger Clough refers in Chapter 2 to a seminal study, first published in 1970, by Isobel Menzies. It was entitled, (a little cumbersome!), *The Functioning of Social Systems as a Defence Against Anxiety* and it used the hospital wards to examine the ways in which 'the system' was organised to protect nurses against the pain and anxiety that their role engendered. Those who are not familiar with the article, or its influence, may think that it is a bit unfair to pick on nurses! In fact, this article has been widely used as an exemplar for comparable organisations, such as residential homes. Menzies examined the way people (including nurses) try to defend themselves against the pain and distress that is generated by getting close to people who are ill, who may die, who will leave us. The intimate tasks which have to be performed place nursing and care staff in a very special position. Menzies showed that at that time certain nursing practices were developed which depersonalised the process, for example, by moving staff around. (It is interesting to note that this has now been officially challenged by the allocation of nurses to specific patients). It reflected a belief that to manage feelings, one had to be impersonal, dispassionate. But this is not a helpful model because the feelings are there: like it or not, they may well up; therefore, the more constructive way forward is to try and deal with them more openly, acknowledging the powerful emotions involved in intimate personal care.

What emerges in discussions such as those at the Lancaster conference is that such caring rôles are deeply stressful and that it is easy to feel 'attacked' from all sides when abuse is debated. It seems important that we identify this and ponder upon it. We need to find allies and supporters, knowing that you will not always be welcomed when you raise matters of abuse. One possibility is to establish networks for support in endeavouring to combat abuse. Indeed one group at the conference toyed with the notion of a kind of lonely hearts column in which 'Anxious registration inspector, slim, 43, male, wishes to meet similarly anxious plump woman with view to mutual learning and support!' (If that sounds too gender specific, it is up to you).

Probably most readers will have a close relative or know someone personally who lives in a home. These issues are real, live and personal. It is not just about work. It is about what we want for those we love and for our own old age. But it is also about our professional integrity and organisational accountability. Perhaps we should, in conclusion, remind ourselves that we can only do so much. There is increasing recognition of burn out in residential staff. But it's not only in the residential staff is it? It is in everybody in this particular world of work. One of the difficulties we may have is that it is such a huge subject. I think all we can do is take a little bit and say, this is the bit I must tackle according to my role and my opportunity. It might be about creating a culture within a residential home of the kind which diminishes the likelihood of abuse. It might be about improving selection procedures for staff. It might be about improving disciplinary procedures with this distinction between the heavy and the light. Thinking about one bit which we can do something about, seems to me to be a helpful way to stop ourselves getting too omnipotent about it and feeling 'It's down to me, it's all too big, I'll go and shoot myself'. Frequently I end reflections of this kind with a Blake quotation. I do know other poems but this one does seem to me extraordinarily apposite! 'He' (or she) 'who would do good must do it in minute particulars.' A few minute particulars will suffice.

Finally a quotation from Jung:

> A human being would certainly not grow to be 70 or 80 years old if this longevity had no meaning for the species. The afternoon of human life must also have a significance of its own and cannot be merely a pitiful appendage to life's morning.

Bibliography

Action on Elder Abuse (1994) *Elder Abuse in Care Homes,* London: Action on Elder Abuse

Action on Elder Abuse Bulletin (1994) Nov/Dec, no. 8, p.1, London: Action on Elder Abuse

Alaszewski A and Manthorpe J (1995) Durkheim, Social Integration and Suicide Rates, *Nursing Times,* 21 June, vol. 91(25), pp.34-35

Alaszewski A and Walsh M (1995) Typologies of Welfare Organisations: A Literature Review, *British Journal of Social Work,* Forthcoming

Allen I, Hogg D and Peace S (1992) *Elderly People: Choice, Participation and Satisfaction,* London: Policy Studies Institute

Arber S and Evandrou M (eds) (1993) *Ageing, Independence and the Life Course,* London: Jessica Kingsley

ARC/NAPSAC (1993) *It Could Never Happen Here! The Prevention and Treatment of Sexual Abuse of Adults with Learning Disabilities in Residential Settings,* Chesterfield and Nottingham: Association for Residential Care and National Association for the Protection from Sexual Abuse of Adults and Children with Learning Disabilities

Audit Commission (1986) *Making a Reality of Community Care*, London: HMSO

Bahr S T (1992) Personhood: A Theory of Gerontological Nursing, *Holistic Nursing Practice,* 7(1), pp.1-6.

Baker D E (1978) *Attitudes of Nurses to the Care of Elderly People,* Manchester: Unpublished PhD Thesis, University of Manchester

Baldwin N, Harris J and Kelly D (1993) Institutionalisation: Why Blame the Institution?, *Ageing & Society,* 13, pp.69-81

Beardshaw V (1981) *Conscientious Objectors at Work,* London: Social Audit

Bennet G (1990) Action on Elder Abuse in the '90s: New Definitions Will Help, *Geriatric Medicine*, 20(4), pp.53-54

Bernard M and Meade K (eds) (1993) *Women Come of Age,* London: Edward Arnold

Biggs S (1993) *Understanding Ageing: Images, Attitudes and Professional Practice*, Buckingham: Open University Press

Bion W (1960) *Experiences in Groups*, London: Tavistock

Bland R, Bland R, Cheetham J, Lapsley I and Revellon S (1992) *Residential Care for Elderly People: Their Costs and Quality*, Edinburgh: HMSO

Blom-Cooper L (1992) *Report of the Committee of Inquiry into Complaints about Ashworth Hospital,* London, HMSO

Bond J and Bond S (1987) Developments in the Evaluation of Long-Term Care for Dependent Old People, in Fielding P (ed), pp.47-86

Brammer A (1994) The Registered Homes Act 1984: Safeguarding the Elderly?, *Journal of Social Welfare and Family Law,* 4, pp.423-437

Brown H (in press) *Towards Better Interviewing: A Handbook on the Sexual Abuse of Adults with Learning Disabilities for Police Officers and Social Workers,* NAPSAC/Tizard 'Need to Know' Series, Brighton: Pavilion Publishing

Brown H (in press) *Towards Better Safeguards: A Handbook on the Sexual Abuse of Adults with Learning Disabilities for Inspectors and Registration Officers,* NAPSAC/Tizard "Need to Know" Series, Brighton: Pavilion Publishing

Brown H and Turk V (1992) Defining Sexual Abuse as it Affects Adults with Learning Disabilities, *Mental Handicap* 20(2), pp.44-55

Brown H, Stein J and Turk V (1995) The Sexual Abuse of Adults with Learning Disabilities: Report of a second 2 year incidence survey, *Mental Handicap Research,* 8(1), pp.1-22

Buchanan A and Oliver J (1977) Abuse and Neglect as a Cause of Mental Retardation: A Study of 140 Children Admitted to Subnormality Hospitals in Wiltshire, *British Journal of Psychiatry,* 131, pp.458-467

Callahan J J (1988) Elder Abuse: Some Questions for Policy Makers', *The Gerontologist,* 28(4), p.453

Care Sector Consortium (1992) *National Occupation Standards For Care,* London: HMSO

Care Weekly (1995) Comment: Breathing Space for Whistle-Blowers, *Care Weekly,* 29 June, p.2

Care Weekly (1995) More Protection for Whistle-Blowers, *Care Weekly,* 13 July, p.3

CARIE (Coalition of advocates for the rights of the infirm elderly) (1991) *Ensuring an Abuse-Free Environment: A Learning Program for Nursing Home Staff,* Philadelphia: Carie

Carr K K and Kazanowski M K (1994) Factors Affecting Job Satisfaction of Nurses Who Work in Long Term Care, *Journal of Advanced Nursing*, 19, pp.878-883

Cassidy J (1995) Home Sick, *Nursing Times*, 91(20), 17 May, pp.20-21

Cervi B (1995) Making Waves, *Community Care,* 28 July, pp.22-23

Challis L and Bartlett H (1988) *Old and Ill: Private Nursing Homes for Elderly People*, London: Age Concern Institute of Gerontology, Research Paper No. 1, ACE Books.

Challis L and Bartlett H (1988) *Old and Ill,* Age Concern England

Chenitz W C (1983) Entry to a Nursing Home as Status Passage: A

Theory to Guide Nursing Practice, *Geriatric Nursing,* March/ April, pp.92-97

Cloake E (1989) Report of Confidential Enquires into Maternal Deaths in England and Wales, 1982-84 : A Summary of the Main Points, *Health Trends,* 21, August, pp.84-85

Clough R (1981) *Old Age Homes,* London: Allen and Unwin

Clough R (1988) Danger: Look Out For Abuse, *Care Weekly,* 29 January.

Clough R (1988) *Scandals in Residential Centres: A Report to the Wagner Committee,* Unpublished

Clough R (ed) (1994) *Insights into Inspection: The Regulation of Social Care,* London: Whiting and Birch

Clough R (1982) *Residential Work,* London: BASW/Macmillan

Clough R (ed) (1995) *Elder Abuse and the Law,* London: Action on Elder Abuse

Community Care (1995) Ashworth Whistle-Blower Wins Industrial Tribunal, *Community Care,* 8 June, p.3

Community Care (1995) Whistle-Blower Researcher, *Community Care,* 23 February, p.4

Community Care Market News (1995), 2(3), June

Copp L (ed) (1981) *In Care of the Ageing,* Edinburgh: Churchill Livingstone

Counsel and Care (1992) *What If They Hurt Themselves,* London: Counsel and Care

Counsel and Care (1991) *No Such Private Places,* London: Counsel and Care

Counsel and Care (1994) *Older People at Risk of Abuse in a Residential Setting*, Fact Sheet No 2, London: Counsel and Care

Craft A (1994) History of 'Knowing': Physical and Sexual Abuse of Adults with Learning Disabilities in Harris, J and Craft, A (eds) (1994)

Crump A (1991) Promoting Self-Esteem, *Nursing the Elderly*, 3, pp.19-21

Dale C, Rae M and Tarbuck P (1995) Changing the Nursing Culture in a Special Hospital, *Nursing Times,* 91(30), 26 July, pp.33-35

Darton R and Wright K (1993) Changes in the Provision of Long-Stay Care 1970-1990, *Journal of Health and Social Care in the Community,* 1(1), January, pp.11-25

Day P and Klein R (1990) *Inspecting the Inspectorates,* York: Joseph Rowntree Memorial Trust

Decalmer P and Glendenning F (eds) (1993) *The Mistreatment of Elderly People*, London: Sage

Dellasega C and Mastrian K (1995) The Process and Consequences of Institutionalising an Elder, *Western Journal of Nursing Research,*

17(2), pp.123-140

Department of Health (1989) *Caring for People,* London: HMSO

Department of Health (1992) *National Assistance Act 1948 (Choice of Accommodation) Directions 1992*, LAC(92)27), London: HMSO

Department of Health (1995) *Charging for Residential Accommodation Guide* (CRAG) Amendment No. 5, LAC(95)7, London, HMSO

Department of Health/Social Services Inspectorate (1989) *Homes Are for Living In*, London: HMSO

Department of Health/Social Services Inspectorate (1990) *Guidance on Standards for Residential Homes for Elderly People*, London: HMSO

Diamond L and Jaudes P (1983) Child Abuse in a Cerebral-Palsied Population, *Developmental Medicine and Child Neurology,* 25, pp.169-174

Dimond T (1986) Social Policy and Everyday Life in Nursing Homes: A Critical Ethnography, *Social Science and Medicine,* 23(12), pp.1287-1295

Dixon B and Hamill R (1994) *The Sonas Approach to Care: Benefits for Elderly People and Development of Staff,* Paper given at International Nursing Conference, University of Ulster, Ulster, 29-31 August 1994

Dooghe G (1992) *The Ageing of the Population in Europe: Socio-Economic Characteristics of Elderly People,* Commission of the European Communities: Brussels

Doty P and Sullivan E W (1983) Community Involvement in Combating Abuse, Neglect and Mistreatment in Nursing Homes, *Milbank Fund Quarterly / Health and Society,* 32, pp.222-251

Eastley R J, MacPherson R, Richards H and Mia I H (1993) Assaults on Professional Carers of Elderly People, *British Medical Journal,* 307, p.845

Eastman M (ed) (1994) *Old Age Abuse: A New Perspective,* London: Chapman and Hall

EBS Trust (1994), *Some Like It Hotter: Handling Complaints in Residential Care,* London: DOH

Evers H K (1981a) Tender Loving Care: Patients and Nurses in Geriatric Wards in Copp L (ed) (1981)

Evers H K (1981b) Multi-Disciplinary Teams in Geriatric Wards: Myth or Reality?, *Journal of Advanced Nursing,* 6, pp.205-214

Evers H K (1982) Professional Practice and Patient Care: Multi-Disciplinary Teams in Geriatric Wards, *Ageing and Society,* 15a, pp.581-588

Fader A, Koge N, Gupta K L and Gambert S R (1990) Perceptions of Elder Abuse by Health Care Workers in a Long-Term Care Setting', *Clinical Gerontologist,* 10(2), pp.87-89

Fielding P (ed) (1987) *Research in the Nursing of Elderly People,* London: John Wiley

Foner N (1994) Nursing Home Aides: Saints or Monsters?, *The Gerontologist,* 34(2), pp.245-250

Forbes (1994) Hope: An Essential Human Need in the Elderly, *Journal of Gerontological Nursing*, 20(6), pp.5-10

Fry A (1992) The Tip of the Iceberg?, *Nursing Times,* 26(88), pp.35, 18

Gair G and Hartery T (1994) Old Peoples' Homes: Residents' Views, *BASELINE (Journal of the British Association for Services to the Elderly),* 54, pp.24-27

Gilleard C (1994) Physical Abuse in Homes and Hospitals in Eastman M (ed) (1994)

Gilloran A J, McGlew T, McKee K, Robertson A and Wight D (1993) Measuring the Quality of Care on Psychogeriatric Wards, *Journal of Advanced Nursing*, 18, pp.269-275

Goffman E (1968) *Asylums*, Harmondsworth: Penguin

Goldstein S and Blank A (1982) The Elderly: Abused or Abusers?', *Canadian Medical Association Journal,* 127, pp.455-456

Goodwin S (1992) Freedom to Care, *Nursing Times,* 88(34), pp.38-39

Guardian (1990) Yours Sincerely, F. G. Pink *Guardian Society Supplement*, 11 April, p.21

Halamandaris V J (1983) Fraud and Abuse in Nursing Homes in Kosberg J I (ed) (1983)

Harman H and Harman S (1989) *No Place Like Home: A Report of the First Ninety-Six Cases of the Registered Homes Tribunal,* London: NALGO

Harris J and Craft A (eds) (1994) *People with Learning Disabilities at Risk of Physical or Sexual Abuse*, BILD Seminar Papers No. 4. Kidderminster: British Institute of Learning Disabilities

Higgs P and Victor C (1993) Institutional Care and the Life Course in Arber S and Evandrou M (eds) (1993)

Higham P (1994) *Individualising Residential Care for Older People*, Paper given at BSG Annual Conference, University of London, September 1994

Hillyard-Parker H et al (1993) *How to Manage Your Training,* London: NISW & NEC

Holmes B and Johnson A (1988) *Cold Comfort: The Scandal of Private Rest Homes,* London: Souvenir Press

Holt M (1995) Looking after Uncle Sam, *Community Care,* 16-22 March

Hood CC et al (1992) Risk Management in Royal Society Study Group (ed) (1992)

Hudson J E (1988) Elder Abuse: An Overview in Schlesinger B and Schlesinger R (eds) (1988)

Hunt G (ed) (1995) *Whistle-Blowing in the Health Service,* London: Edward Arnold

Hunter S, Brace S and Buckley G (1993) *The Inter-Disciplinary Assessment of Older People at Entry into Long-Term Institutional Care: Lessons for the New Community Care Arrangements*

The Independent (1994) The Cruelty That Thrives on Secrecy, *The Independent,* 17 September, London

Jacelon C S (1995) The Effects of Living in a Nursing Home on Socialisation in Elderly People, *Journal of Advanced Nursing,* 22(3), pp.539-546

Janforum (1985) Present and Future Care of the Elderly, *Journal of Advanced Nursing,* 10, pp.491-496

Johnson M (1995) *Ethical Aspects of Allocation of Resources to Elderly People,* Milton Keynes: Open University

Johnson R A, Schwiebert V B and Rosenmann P A (1994) Factors Influencing Nursing Home Placement Decisions, *Clinical Nursing Research,* 3(3), pp.269-281

Jones G et al (1993) *Avoiding Restraint in Residential Care for Older People*, Unpublished, Hampshire County Council

Jones R (1993), *Registered Homes Act Manual*, London: Sweet & Maxwell

Kadner K (1994) Therapeutic Intimacy in Nursing, *Journal of Advanced Nursing*, 19(2), pp.215-218

Kayser-Jones J (1990) *Old, Alone and Neglected: Care of the Aged in the United States and Scotland,* Los Angeles: University of California Press, Second Edition

Kayser-Jones J S (1981/1990) *Old and Alone, Care of the Aged in the UK and Scotland,* Berkeley: University of California Press

Kellaher L and Peace S (1990) *From Respondent to Consumer to Resident: Shifts in Quality Assurance in the Last Decade*, Paper given at BSG Annual Conference, University of Durham 1990

Kenny T (1990) Erosion of Individuality in Care of Elderly People in Hospital: An Alternative Approach, *Journal of Advanced Nursing,* 15, pp.571-576

Kimsey L R, Tarbox A R and Bragg D F (1981) Abuse of the Elderly: The Hidden Agenda 1. The Caretakers and the Categories of Abuse, *American Geriatrics Society Journal,* 29, pp.465-472

Kingston P and Penhale B (eds) (1995) *Family Violence and the Caring Professions,* London: Macmillan

Kitson A L (1986) Indicators of Quality in Nursing Care: An Alternative Approach, *Journal of Advanced Nursing,* 11, pp.133-144

Koch T, Weth C and Williams A M (1995) Listening to the Voices of

Older Patients: An Excitential-Phenominological Approach to Quality Assurance, *Journal of Clinical Nursing,* 4, pp.185-193

Kosberg J I (ed) (1983) *Abuse and Maltreatment of the Elderly: Causes and Interventions,* Boston: John Wright

Kuremyr D, Kihlgren M, Norberg A, Aström S and Karlsson K (1994) Emotional Experience, Empathy and Burnout Among Staff Caring for Patients at a Collective Living Unit and Nursing Home, 19(4), January, pp.670-679

Kyle T U (1995) The Concept of Caring: A Literature Review, *Journal of Advanced Nursing,* 21(3), pp.506-514

Lachs M S, Berkman L, Fulmer T and Horwitz R I (1994) A Prospective Community-Based Pilot Study of Risk Factors for the Investigation of Elder Mistreatment, *Journal of the American Geriatrics Society,* 42, pp.169-173

Laczko F and Victor C (eds) (1992) *Social Policy and Elderly People,* Aldershot: Gower

Law Commission (1993) *Mentally Incapacitated and Other Vulnerable Adults: Public Law Protection,* Consultation Paper No. 130, London: HMSO

Law Commission (1995) *Mental Incapacity*, Consultation Paper No. 231, London: HMSO

Lawrence S, Walker A and Willcocks D (1977) *She's Leaving Home: Local Authority Policy and Practice Concerning Admissions into Residential Homes for Old People*, CESSA Research Report No 2, London: Polytechnic of North London

Lawton M P, Moss M and Duhamel L M (1995) The Quality of Life Among Elderly Care Persons, *Journal of Applied Gerontology,* 14(2), pp.150-171

Lee-Treweek G (1993) *Bedrooms, Nursing Auxiliaries and Order in a Nursing Home*, Xeroxed Conference Paper, Norwich: Department of Applied Social Science, University of East Anglia

Lee-Treweek G (1994) Bedroom Abuse: The Hidden Work in a Nursing Home, *Generations Review,* 4(1), March

Lowenstein A and Brick Y *The Differential and Congruent Roles of Qualitative and Quantitative Methods To Evaluate Quality of Life in Residential Settings,* Israeli Gerontological Society, Israel

Lyon, C and Ashcroft (1994) *Legal Issues Arising from the Care and Control of Children with Learning Disabilities Who Also Present Severe Challenging Behaviour,* London: The Mental Health Foundation

Manthorpe J (1993) Social Work and Elder Abuse in Decalmer P and Glendenning F (eds) (1993)

Marck P (1990) Therapeutic Reciprocity: A Caring Phenomenon *Advances in Nursing Science*, 13(1), pp.49-59

Martin J, Meltzer H and Elliott D (1988) *OPCS Survey of Disability in Great Britain, Report 1 Prevalence of Disability Among Adults*, London: HMSO

Martin J P (1984) *Hospitals in Trouble,* Oxford: Blackwell

Maslach C (1982) *Burn-Out: The Cost of Caring,* Englewood Cliffs, NJ: Prentice-Hall

McCreadie C (1991) *Elder Abuse: An Exploratory Study,* London: Age Concern Institute of Gerontology

McFarlane J K (1976) A Charter for Nursing *Journal of Advanced Nursing,* 1, pp.187-196

Menzies I (1970) *The Functioning of Social Systems as a Defence Against Anxiety*, London: Tavistock Institute of Human Relations

Miller E J and Gwynne G V (1972) *A Life Apart: A Pilot Study of Residential Institutions for the Physically Handicapped and the Young,* London: Tavistock

Miller L (1995) *Validation Therapy: The Human Face of Elderly Care?* Paper given at BSG Annual Conference, University of Keele 1995

Monk A, Kaye L W and Litwin H (1984) *Resolving Grievances in the Nursing Home: A Study of the Ombudsman's Program,* New York: Columbia University Press

Morris I (1994), *The Shape of Things to Come,* London: NISW

Morse J M, Solberg S M, Neander W L, Bottroff J L and Johnson J L (1990) Concepts of Caring and Caring as a Concept, *Advances in Nursing Sciences*, 13(1), pp.1-14

NALGO (1989) *No Place Like Home,* London: NALGO

Neill J (1989) *Assessing People for Residential Care: A Practical Guide,* London: National Institute of Social Work Research Unit

Newbern V B and Krowchuck H U (1994) Failure to Thrive in Elderly People: A Conceptual Analysis, *Journal of Advanced Nursing*, 99(5), pp.840-849

Nolan M R, Grant G and Nolan J (1995) Busy Doing Nothing: Activity and Interaction Levels Amongst Differing Populations of Elderly Patients, *Journal of Advanced Nursing,* 22(3), pp.528-539

Nolan M R (1987) *Is Nursing Throwing the Patient Out with the Bath Water: An Analysis of Consumer and Professional Perspectives on a Nursing Service for the Disabled and Elderly?,* International Conference in Pursuit of Excellence, Royal College of Nursing, London, November 1987

Nolan M R and Grant G (1993) Rust Out a Therapeutic Reciprocity: Concepts to Advance the Nursing Care of Elderly People, *Journal of Advanced Nursing,* 18, pp.1305-1314

Norton D, McClaren R and Exton-Smith A N (1962) *An Investigation into Geriatric Nursing Problems in Hospital*, Research Report

NCCOP (reprinted 1979), Edinburgh: Churchill Livingston

Osborne J and Stott M (1993) Unpublished papers on the investigation of abuse in homes for older people

Parker H (ed) and Oldfield N, Thirlway M, Nelson M and Hutton S (1995) *Modest But Adequate? Modest-But-Adequate Budgets for Four Pensioner Households,* London: Age Concern, England

Parker R (1990) Private Residential Homes and Nursing Homes in Sinclair I, Parker R, Leat D and Williams J (eds) (1990)

Patel U (1994) *The Group Self,* Unpublished Paper, Bombay

Payne C (1994), *Evaluating the Quality of Care,* London: NISW

Payton V and Reed J (1995) *Making the Stranger Seem Familiar: Coping with Institutional Life,* Newcastle-upon-Tyne: Centre for Health Services, The University of Newcastle-upon-Tyne

Peace S (1993) The Living Environments of Older Women in Bernard M and Meade K (eds) (1993)

Pennington R E and Pierce W L (1985) Observations of Empathy of Nursing-Home Staff: A Predictive Study International, *Journal of Aging and Human Development,* 21(4), pp.281-290

Phillipson C (1993) Abuse of Older People: Sociological Perspectives in Decalmer P and Glendenning F (eds) (1993)

Phillipson C and Biggs S (1992) *Understanding Elder Abuse: A Training Manual for Helping Professionals,* Harlow: Longman Group UK

Phillipson C and Biggs S (1995) Elder Abuse: A Critical Overview in Kingston P and Penhale B (eds) (1995)

Phillipson C and Walker A (eds) (1986) *Ageing and Social Policy: A Critical Assessment,* Aldershot: Gower

Pilgrim, D. (1995) Explaining Abuse and Inadequate Care in Hunt, G. (1995) (ed)

Pillemer K (1988) Maltreatment of Patients in Nursing Homes: Overview and Research Agenda, *Journal of Health and Social Behavior,* 29(3), pp.227-238

Pillemer K and Bachman-Prehn (1991) Helping and Hurting: Predictors of Maltreatment of Patients in Nursing Homes, *Research on Aging,* 13(1), pp.74-95

Pillemer K and Hudson B (1993) A Model Abuse Prevention Program for Nursing Assistants, *The Gerontologist,* 33(1), pp.128-131

Pillemer K and Lachs M S (1995) Abuse and Neglect of Elderly Persons, *The New England Journal of Medicine,* 332(7), pp.437-443

Pillemer K and Moore D W (1989) Abuse of Patients in Nursing Home: Findings From a Survey of Staff, *The Gerontologist,* 29(3), pp.314-320

Pillemer K and Moore D W (1990) Highlights from a Study of Abuse in Nursing Homes, *Journal of Elder Abuse and Neglect,* 2(1/2), pp.5-

29
Poole G and Rowat K (1994) Elderly Clients' Perceptions of a Caring Home-Care Nurse, *Journal of Advanced Nursing,* 20(3), pp.422-429

Porter E J and Clinton J F (1992) Adjusting to the Nursing Home, Western *Journal of Nursing Research*, 14(4), pp.464-481

Potier M and Ghosh C (1995) Ashworth Dismissal Not a Ploy to Stop Whistleblowers, Letter, *Community Care,* 22 June, p.12

Pottage D and Evans M (1994) *The Competent Workplace : The View from Within,* London: NISW

Pritchard J (1995) *The Abuse of Older People,* London: Jessica Kingsley

Public Concern at Work (1995) *Concerns at Work*, London: Public Concern at Work

Pursey A and Luker K (1995) Attitudes and Stereotypes: Nurses Work with Older People; *Journal of Advanced Nursing,* 22, pp.547-555

Radsman J (1994) Caring and Nursing: A Dilemma, *Journal of Advanced Nursing,* 20(3), pp.444-449

Reed J and Bond S (1991) Nurses' Assessment of Elderly Patients in Hospital, *International Journal of Nursing Studies,* 28(1), pp.55-64

Reed J and MacMillan J (1994) *Settling In: Ways of Adapting to Life in Nursing and Residential Homes for Older People,* Paper given at BSG Annual Conference, University of London, September 1994

Reed J and Payton V *Accomplishing Friendships in Nursing and Residential Homes,* Centre for Health Services Research, The University of Newcastle-upon-Tyne

Registered Homes Tribunal (1993) *Davies v. Powys County Council*, Decision 221, Registered Homes Tribunal

Reinhardy J R (1992) Decisional Control in Moving into a Nursing Home; Post-Admission Adjustment and Well-Being, *Gerontologist*, 32(1), pp.96-103

Research, Policy and Planning, 11(1/2), pp.2-9

Robb B (1967) *Sans Everything: A Case to Answer,* Edinburgh: Nelson

Robb S S (1984) Behaviour in the Environment of the Elderly in Yurick A G, Spier B E, Robb S S and Ebert N J (eds) (1984)

Roberts S, Steele J and Morse N (1991) *Finding Out About Residential Care: Results of a Survey of Users*, Working Paper 3, London: Policy Studies Institute

Rosswurm M A (1983) Relocation and the Elderly, *Journal of Gerontological Nursing,* 9(12), pp.632-637

Royal College of Nursing (1992) *A Scandal Waiting to Happen? Elderly People and Nursing Care in Residential and Nursing Homes,*

Royal College of Nursing, London

Royal Society Study Group (ed) (1992) *Risk, Analysis, Perception and Management*, London: The Royal Society

Rusch R, Hall J and Griffin H (1986) Abuse-Provoking Characteristics of Institutionalised Mentally Retarded Individuals, *American Journal of Mental Deficiency,* 90(6), pp.618-624

Sarton M (1983) *As We Are Now,* London: The Women's Press Ltd

Schlesinger B and Schlesinger R (1988) *Abuse of the Elderly: Issues and Annotated Bibliography,* Toronto: University of Toronto Press

Schulz R and Brenner G (1977) Relation of the Aged: A Review and Theoretical Analysis, *Journal of Gerontology*, 32(3), pp.323-333.

Scott P A (1995) Care, Attention and Imaginative Identification in Nursing Practice, *Journal of Advanced Nursing,* 21(6), pp.1196-1200

Shaw C, Hurst M and Stone S (1988) *Towards Good Practices in Small Hospitals - Some Suggested Guidelines,* Birmingham: National Association of Health Authorities

Sinclair I (1990) Residential Care in Sinclair I, Parker R, Leat D and Williams J (eds) (1990)

Sinclair I (ed) (1988a) *Residential Care: The Research Reviewed,* Vol. 2 of the Wagner Committee Report, London: HMSO

Sinclair I et al (1988b) *Bridging Two Worlds: Social Work and the Elderly Living Alone,* Aldershot: Avebury

Sinclair I, Parker P, Leat D and Williams J (eds) (1990) *The Kaleidoscope of Care: A Review of Research on Welfare Provision for Elderly People,* London: HMSO

Smale G (1992) *Managing Change Through Innovation,* London: NISW

Smith G and Cantley C (1985) *Assessing Health Care,* Buckingham: Open University Press

Solomon, K (1983) Intervention for Victimised Elderly and Sensitisation of Health Professionals in Kosberg J (ed) (1983)

Southwark Social Services (1987) *Report of the Inquiry into Nye Bevan Lodge,* London: London Borough of Southwark

Southwark Social Services Department (1995) *Challenging Bad Practice at Work,* London: London Borough of Southwark

Stannard C (1973) Old Folks and Dirty Work: The Social Conditions for Patient Abuse in a Nursing Home, *Social Problems,* 20, pp.329-342

Stathopoulos P (1983) Consumer Advocacy and Abuse of Elders in Nursing Homes in Kosberg J (ed) (1983)

Stevenson O (1972) *Strength and Weakness in Residential Care,* Quetta Rabley Memorial Lecture

Stone K (1995) Whistle Down The Wind, *Community Care,* 6-12 July, pp.16-17

Sumaya-Smith I (1995) Caregiver - Resident Relationships: Surrogate Family Bonds and Surrogate Grieving in a Skilled Nursing Facility, *Journal of Advanced Nursing*, 21(3), pp.447-451

Sundram C (1984) Obstacles to Reducing Patient Abuse in Public Institutions, *Hospital and Community Psychiatry,* 35(3), pp.238-243

Tarbox A R (1983) The Elderly in Nursing Homes: Psychological Aspects of Neglect, *Clinical Gerontologist,* 1, pp.39-52

Tellis-Nayak V and Tellis-Nayak M (1979) Quality of Care and the Burden of Two Cultures: When the World of the Nurse's Aide Enters the World of the Nursing Home, *The Gerontologist,* 29, pp.307-313

The National Health Service and Community Care Act, 1990, London: HMSO

Tomlin S (1989) *Abuse of Elderly People: An Unnecessary and Preventable Problem,* London: British Geriatrics Society

Townsend P (1962) *The Last Refuge* , London: Routledge and Kegan Paul

Townsend P and Davidson N (1982) *Inequalities in Health: The Black Report,* Harmondsworth: Penguin Books

Turk V and Brown H (1993) The Sexual Abuse of Adults with Learning Disabilities: Results of a Two Year Incidence Survey, *Mental Handicap Research,* 6(3), pp.193-216

Turner P (1993) Activity Nursing and the Changes in the Quality of Life of Elderly Patients: A Semi-Quantitative Study, *Journal of Advanced Nursing,* 19, pp.239-248

Turner P (1994) *Creative Therapeutic Activity Programmes for All Health and Social Care Settings,* Paper given at International Nursing Conference, University of Ulster, 29-31 August 1994

UKCC (United Kingdom Central Council for Nursing, Midwifery and Health Visiting) (1994) *Professional Conduct: Occasional Report on Standards of Nursing in Nursing Homes,* London: UKCC

Victor C (1992) Do We Need Institutional Care? in Laczko F and Victor C (eds) (1992)

Vousden M (1987) Nye Bevan Would Turn in His Grave, *Nursing Times,* 83(32), pp.18-19

Wagner Committee (1988) *Residential Care: A Positive Choice* , *Report of the Independent Review of Residential Care,* Vol. 1, London: HMSO

Wagner Development Group (1991) *Inside Quality Assurance,* London: CESSA

Walker A, Alber J and Guillemard A M (eds) (1993) *Older People in Europe: Social and Economic Policies: The 1993 Report of the*

European Observatory, Brussels: Commission of the European Communities

Wardhaugh J and Wilding P (1993) Towards an Explanation of the Corruption of Care, *Critical Social Policy,* 47, pp.4-31

Warner N (1992) *Choosing with Care: The Report of the Committee of Inquiry into the Selection, Development and Management of Staff in Children's Homes,* London: HMSO

Waters K (1994) Getting Dressed in the Morning: Styles of Staff/ Patients Interaction on Rehabilitation Hospital Wards for Elderly People, *Journal of Advanced Nursing,* 19, pp.239-248

Wells T J (1980) *Problems in Geriatric Nursing,* Edinburgh: Churchill Livingstone

Westcott, H (1993) *Abuse of Children and Adults with Disabilities*, Policy, Practice, Research Series, London: NSPCC

Wiener C L and Kayser-Jones J (1990) The Uneasy Fate of Nursing Home Residents: An Organisational-Interaction Perspective', *Sociology of Health and Illness,* 12(1), pp.84-104

Willcocks D, Peace S and Kellaher L (1987) *Private Lives in Public Places,* London: Tavistock

Willcocks D (1986) Residential Care in Phillipson C and Walker A (eds) (1986)

Williams C (1993) Vulnerable Victims? A Current Awareness of the Victimisation of People with Learning Disabilities, *Disability, Handicap and Society,* 8(2), pp.161-172

Yurick A G, Spier B E, Robb S S and Ebert N J (eds) (1984) *The Aged Person and the Nursing Process*, Connecticut: Appleton-Century-Crofts

Notes on Contributors

Dick Clough is the first full-time General Secretary of the Social Care Association, a post he has held since 1978. Before he took up the post he worked in residential child care. He was a member of the working group that produced *Home Life*. Currently he chairs the working party from the Residential Forum which is producing a guide to standards in residential care for adults. He has acted as adviser/consultant to the Department of Health and the Welsh Office. In addition he has chaired or been involved in seven independent inquiries into standards of residential care and frequently has been called as an expert witness in tribunal or High Court actions. He was awarded the MBE in 1979 and the OBE in 1993 for his services to residential care.

Roger Clough is Professor of Social Work, Lancaster University, having moved from the post of Chief Inspector of Social Services with Cumbria Social Services. He started work as a teacher/housemaster in senior boys approved schools, from there he moved to social work teaching, spending 20 years at Bristol Polytechnic and University, specialising in residential work, He was a county councillor for 8 years, including being Chair of the Social Services Committee. He is a member of the Residential Forum, the newly established body to take on the work of Wagner, Warner and Utting. His overriding interest has been in understanding and developing practice in residential work. His publications include: *Old Age Homes; Residential Work; Practice, Power and Politics in Social Services Departments; Insights into Inspection: The Regulation of Social Care* (editor); *Groups and Groupings: Life and Work in Day and Residential Centres* (with A. Brown); and forthcoming *Care in Chaos* (R. Hadley).

Ann Craft is a Senior Lecturer, Department of Learning Disabilities, University of Nottingham Medical School. She has written extensively on the subject of sexuality and individuals with learning disabilities. She has developed health and sex education material for students with learning difficulties, the most recent being 'Living Your Life: A Sex Education and Personal Development Programme for Students with Severe Learning Difficulties', published by LDA in 1991. Her current research project, funded by the Joseph Rowntree Foundation, concerns sexuality and individuals with profound and multiple impairment. She is the co-author (with Hilary Brown) of *Working with the 'Unthinkable'* (FPA, 1992), joint editor of *Thinking the Unthinkable* (FPA, 1989) and editor of *Practice Issues in Sexuality and Learning Disabilities* (Routledge, 1994). Ann Craft is also the Director of the National Association for the Protection from Sexual Abuse of Adults and Children with Learning Disabilities (NAPSAC). NAPSAC is a support and information network for those in learning disability services. It publishes a quarterly Bulletin and an Annotated Bibliography.

Lorayne Ferguson has been working in services for elderly people since 1977, first as a hospital based social worker and then as an area based elderly specialist. For four years from 1988 she was Manager, Holybourne Day Centre, London Borough of Wandsworth, a recognised training resource and model of care for those with a dementing illness. Since 1982 she has been a manager of residential, domiciliary and day care resources in Kent, and continues in training and evaluation activities.

Frank Glendenning is an Honorary Senior Research Fellow in Social Gerontology, Keele University and in Educational Gerontology, Lancaster University. In the early 1990s, he became a Visiting Professor, Department of Health Studies and Gerontology, Waterloo University, Ontario. After spending most of his career in adult education at Keele, he retired seven years ago and since then has travelled widely, lecturing on ageing and gerontological issues in Australia, Belgium, Canada, Finland, and Holland. He is editor of *Baseline,* the journal of the British Association for Service to the Elderly and joint editor of *Education and Ageing*. With Peter Decalmer, he produced the first theoretical text in the UK on *The Mistreatment of Elderly People* (Sage, 1993) which is to be published in Japanese later this year. He has edited and contributed to a book on *Learning and Cognition in Later Life*, to be published by Arena later this year, and is the author of many published articles on social and educational gerontology. He is a former chair, Beth Johnson Foundation and is currently chair, Stoke-on-Trent Council for Voluntary Service.

Elisabeth Henderson is an organisational development consultant working with the management of change and major internal or external re-organisation. Her consultancy is international: Poland (advising the creation and consolidation of the Ministry of Privatisation), India, The Netherlands, the USA, as well as Britain. She trained in adult psychotherapy at the Tavistock Institute, where she became interested in socio-technical systems and the connection between personal and professional development. Following this she founded the Recess College, an Anglo-Dutch initiative for senior professionals and executives. The College supports people of influence to re-appraise their own approach to the dimension of leadership and personal and professional renewal. In relation to this paper she worked with John Osborne and Mandy Stott.

Hazel Ker is a freelance training consultant based in the East Midlands. The main focus of her work is in management development both with teams and individuals; personal and professional counselling; and designing and delivering training in many aspects of social care. Her background is in residential work and management within Social Services and Youth Treatment Centres.

Mark Lymbery is Lecturer in Social Work, School of Social Studies, University of Nottingham, with responsibility for teaching on adult and community care. He was formerly Community Care Implementation Officer in Nottinghamshire Social Services Department.

George Mabon has chaired local and national provider organisations, is a Governor of the National Institute for Social Work, and worked on the Wagner Development Group. He was a founder member of the Residential Forum and is involved in the implementation group for the proposed General Social Services Council.

Jill Manthorpe is Lecturer in Community Care, University of Hull. She has published widely in the area of welfare services for older people and has a long-standing interest in policies and practice around the area of elder abuse and neglect.

Evelyn McEwen, Director of Information for Age Concern England has been with the charity for 14 years. She is responsible for information services to the public and policy development for the organisation. She has also been a member of both a local and a health authority.

Mike Nolan trained as a teacher in the mid 1970s before joining the nursing profession, where he has experience as a clinician, teacher and researcher. For the past 12 years he has been interested in the health and support needs of older people and their carers, with an emphasis on service development and evaluation. He has published widely on a number of topics, particularly relating to the needs of family carers.

John Osborne is manager and joint owner of 'At Your Service' a home support company based in Nottingham. Prior to this he was Service Manager (Older People) with Social Services. He has worked on behalf of the Overseas Development Agency on developing older peoples services in the Czech Republic. He has designed and delivered various training programmes, including on elder abuse staff in practice and has provided inputs to qualifying training at universities and further education colleges.

Olive Stevenson is Emeritus Professor, Social Work Studies, University of Northampton. She has long standing interests in the personal social services and has researched and published on the social care of frail elderly people.

Anni Zlotnick arrived from the USA seven years ago. Her background includes 15 successful years in the field of health care and social care in New York and Connecticut where she managed and administered both community and hospital based programmes. Her management skills were called upon to provide training, mentoring, and coaching for a wide range of staff. Armed with degrees in Psychology, Counselling (Masters Degree), and Social Work, Annie formed a consortium of trainers upon her arrival in the UK. She now specialises in management and process consulting, with specialist training in issues around adult (elder) abuse.

Subject Index

Name Index